Exploring the Ancient Book of
Genesis

Exploring the Ancient Book of
Genesis

How the World Began, How It All Got Ruined and How God Began His Amazing Plan of Redemption

14 Bible Studies for Individual or Group Meditation

Mark and Maryanna Lanford

Exploring the Ancient Book of Genesis is part of a series of Bible study and devotional books from *Life Studies for Followers of Jesus*.

Unless otherwise indicated, all Scripture quotations are taken from the Holy Bible, New International Version®, NIV®. Copyright © 1973, 1978, 1984, 2011 by Biblica, Inc.TM Used by permission of Zondervan. All rights reserved worldwide.

The "NIV" and "New International Version" are trademarks registered in the United States Patent and Trademark Office by Biblica, Inc.™

Note: All emphases included in scripture quotations are the author's additions.

Scripture quotations marked ESV are from The ESV® Bible (The Holy Bible, English Standard Version®), copyright © 2001 by Crossway, a publishing ministry of Good News Publishers. Used by permission. All rights reserved

ISBN Paperback:979-8-9906834-6-4
First Edition © 2014 Life Resources
Second Edition © 2025 Life Resources

Other books from *LIFE STUDIES for Followers of Jesus*:
- *50 Life Studies from the Teachings of Jesus the Messiah*
- *Growing in Christ through the Beatitudes*
- *One Flesh-One Heart*, for married or engaged couples
- *Raising Children to Walk with God*, for parents
- *Following Jesus Together: A Guide for Christians Who Meet in Homes*
- *Discover the Greatness of God through the Miracles of Jesus*

All of these books are available for free download in pdf or epub format in many languages at: *www.learnhisways.com*

The English version of these books is available in paperback from Amazon.com or Amazon.co.uk.

O Lord, our Lord,
how majestic is your name in all the earth!
You have set your glory above the heavens…
When I consider the heavens, the work of your fingers,
The moon and the stars which you have set in place,
What is man that you are mindful of him,
And the son of man that you care for him?
Yet you have made him a little lower than the heavenly
beings and crowned him with glory and honor.
Psalm 8:1 & 3-5 (ESV)

Table of Contents

Genesis: Laying a Solid Foundation for our Faith 6
How To Use These Studies With a Group or Alone 8
1. Creation: *Genesis 1-2* 10
2. The Fall of Man Into Sin: *Genesis 3* 15
3. Sin Increases on the Earth: *Genesis 4-10* 19
4. The Tower of Babel: *Genesis 11* 24
5. Abraham: God's Call and Covenant: *Genesis 12-15* 28
6. Abraham: the Birth of Ishmael & Isaac: *Genesis 16-21* 35
7. The Destruction of Sodom and Gomorrah: 39
   Genesis 18:16-33 and 19:1-29
8. Abraham Is Tested; Abraham's Death: *Genesis 22-25* 43
9. Jacob: Chosen and Blessed by God: *Part 1, Genesis 25-28* 47
10. Jacob: Chosen and Blessed by God: *Part 2, Genesis 29-35* 51
11. Joseph: a Man of Faith and Forgiveness: 55
    Part 1, Genesis 37 & 39:1-6
12. Joseph: a Man of Faith and Forgiveness: 58
    Part 2, Genesis 39:7-41:57
13. Joseph: a Man of Faith and Forgiveness: 63
    Part 3, Genesis 42-50
14. Overview From Creation to Joseph: *Genesis 1-50* 69
To Do on Your Own 74
Guidelines for Translators 77

GENESIS
LAYING A SOLID FOUNDATION FOR OUR FAITH

Anyone who reads Genesis can see that it is an amazing book. It tells us about the beginning of life in our world. It helps us understand where we came from, and it shows us that human beings have a special relationship with God because He created them in His own image.

Genesis begins with amazing beauty. But soon it shows the beginning and growth of sin in the world. It shows how sin destroys individuals, families and nations. Many people are unaware that in the book of Genesis we find many answers to our questions about why we are here, and why the world is the way it is. It also opens our eyes to a very important fact which brings stability to our lives. This fact is that there is a God who created everything, and He continues to work out His good purposes in spite of the destruction that sin brings. He hates sin and brings judgment against it. But He also is a God with a plan and a purpose to save and bless the world. We need to understand that plan.

If we have no knowledge of our history, or of our ancestors, or if we don't have an accurate picture of what God is really like, we are like a spacecraft drifting aimlessly through space. We are like a large tree with very shallow roots which the winds can easily knock over. But God does not want us to be blind to what He is like and what is happening in this world. As we open Genesis and read it, light and hope come to our minds and hearts.

In Genesis we learn about men of faith who were called by God for His special purposes—men like Adam, Noah, Abraham, Jacob, Joseph, and others. Were they perfect? No. The Bible tells us the truth about the men and women in its pages. They were people just like you and me. But blessing came to men of faith, even though they had many trials and didn't follow the Lord perfectly. Through them God began to build a nation. Through that nation—Israel—God would send the Savior, the Messiah.

These studies are written for followers of Jesus, as you will see in each study. However, people who are not followers of Jesus but are searching for truth, may also gain much from the studies. Jesus, who lived 2,000 years after Abraham, knew the book of Genesis well and talked about it in His teachings. He quoted Genesis 2 when he taught about marriage. He also spoke of Noah, Abraham, Isaac and Jacob. He did not speak of Genesis as a fable. He taught that its people and its truths were rooted in actual history. And so we learn from Jesus that knowing this book is important to all who want to know the one true God. The message of Genesis is strongly connected to the good news of Jesus Christ. Therefore we will sometimes take you to the New Testament to see how Genesis connects with our salvation. The better we understand salvation, the better we will live.

May God richly bless you as you study.

How to Use These Studies with a Group or Alone

These studies are an overview of the book of Genesis. Their purpose is to help you to see the big picture of the book of our beginnings. Therefore, many stories are not looked at in detail. You may want to go back later and look more closely at some of the stories to learn more of the many lessons they have to teach us.

You will notice that there is a lot of reading connected with these studies. In order to get the most out of them, it is best **to read through all 50 chapters of Genesis**. At the end of each lesson in this book, you will see recommended readings for the next study. Before you start that study, take time to read through those chapters at least once. Remember, the Bible passage itself is what you want to learn from. If you are studying with a group, reading the passage before coming to the study will help you to understand what is happening much better. The more familiar you are with the passage being studied, the more you will gain from the questions in this book.

This book has been especially written for small group Bible study... for the home group to use each week when it gathers together, for example. Also, you may want to use it to disciple people at other times during the week.

This book is a guide to help you read Genesis more carefully. In these studies, you will see different types of questions:

- One type of question asks the group to **look carefully at a verse** to make sure that they are not missing important parts of the story.

- A second type of question helps the group to **think about and discuss the meaning of certain verses.** Genesis is rich in helping us understand the meaning of life. Therefore it is good to stop often and contemplate what the writer is trying to tell us. A group that takes time to think about the meaning of the passage will find a spiritual feast each week.

- A third type of question helps the group to **think about how they will apply what they have learned to their lives today.** Don't rush over these questions. Take time to discuss them. And make sure you take time for prayer. This is where your lives will change for the better.

If you are studying this book alone, you may want to write your thoughts down in a notebook. When we are not in a group, we usually don't form our thoughts into words. If, when alone, we write our thoughts down, we become more exact in what we think. Also, we can go back and read our notes at any time in the future. These notes also might be used to teach others.

GROUP LEADERS – Here are some guidelines to make these studies meaningful to every group member:

- **As the group leader, study the passage and questions alone before you meet with the group.** You will be better prepared to help the group members if you yourself are acquainted with the study beforehand.
- **Begin your group study with prayer and faith** that He will be with you to help you understand and obey His word.
- **The most important part of these studies is the Bible passage itself.** As a group, make sure you read the assigned passage at least once.
- **Make sure group members look carefully at the verses before they give their answers.** The studies are designed to discover what the Bible actually teaches, not to guess about what we think it says.
- **Be sure to have the group answer each question, one by one.** There are sometimes three or four questions under one item. Don't read the questions all at once. Give an answer to each question before going on to the next.
- **These studies are made for group discussion, not for anyone to preach or teach the whole lesson.** Try to give everyone in the group the opportunity to briefly share his thoughts on at least a few of the questions. Encourage all to participate and none to dominate the discussion
- **If possible, sit in a circle so group members can see each other.** This will feel more informal than a "classroom" style, with chairs in rows and a leader doing all the teaching up at the front. A circle will help the group members feel more free to participate in the discussion.
- **As much as possible, make sure that everyone has their own copy of the lesson and a Bible.** Encourage group members to take the study home and do it again with their family or friends.

- Some of these studies cover a lot of material or may generate a lot of thoughtful discussion. In this case, **you may find it helpful to take two sessions rather than rushing to complete everything in one sitting**.

Note: Before you begin the first study, read through all of chapters 1&2 of Genesis. If you are studying this book with a group, read these chapters on your own before coming to the group study.

1. CREATION

Genesis 1-2

Opening Questions:

All of us have questions about God. What are some of your unanswered questions about God and the world? Do you think it's possible to find answers to questions about our beginnings?

Introduction:

While the Bible does not tell us everything about the beginning of the universe and our world, there are some very important truths that we can learn from the study of the first few chapters of Genesis. This first study will look at the story of the creation of the world and of mankind.

Read Genesis 1:1-25.

1. Read Genesis 1:1 again.

    This is the very first verse of God's Holy Book, explaining to us how things began. What important truth about creation do we learn from this verse? Think about it. Why do you think this verse is first in the Bible?

Where did God come from?

Most of us ask this question at some point in our lives. But here in Genesis there is no explanation given to us of where God came from. He is already there in the first verse of the Holy Book. So, we can understand that the words "in the beginning" are talking about our beginning, not His beginning. Nowhere in the Old or New Testaments does God tell us about His beginning because He tells us in other chapters of the Bible that He had no beginning and He will have no end. This is a mystery that man cannot understand.

Even though there are mysteries, we will see that God reveals many things about Himself and about our ancient history in this Holy Book. This helps us to better understand what is happening in our world today. We depend on Him to teach us the truth about how to live as He created us to live.

---

2. What words are the same in verses 3, 6, 9, 11, 14, (and other verses of this chapter)?

3. When we read that God created the universe with the words "Let there be..." it speaks powerfully to our hearts. We see that God creates with His word!

   Think about our big world, our very hot sun, and huge galaxies with millions of stars coming into existence because God says, "Let there be..." How does that affect you?

4. How is God's creation described in verses 4, 10, 12, 18, (and other verses)?

The gods of ancient civilizations

Many cultures in the ancient world had mythical stories about how the world began. But the stories about their gods were very different from this story about God in Genesis. Those mythical gods had human weaknesses: they fought each other; they had family arguments, jealousy and strife; they were limited in what they could do; and often they were immoral. But when we read about creation in Genesis we see a very different picture. We see a grand picture of an all-powerful God, creating a world with perfection, beauty, and purpose. After each day of creation, God announces, "It is good."

Today we live in a world filled with sin. But when we read Genesis 1 and 2 we realize that life didn't start out bad—it started out good! Deep in our hearts we know that it should be that way. When we read these chapters, we begin to see a GRAND DESIGN. And so we ask, "What is God's grand design for this world? What does He want for us, His creation?"

Read Genesis 1:26-31 and all of chapter 2.

5. These verses tell about the most majestic part of God's creation. Chapter 1:26-31 tells about the creation of the man and woman. Then, chapter 2:7 and 15-25 gives us more details of their creation.

   What do you think "created in His image" means? (Genesis 1:26-27) Describe your own ideas before you read the section below.

Why is mankind special?

When God created the universe, he did it with His word. However, when He created man, He did it very differently. Read Gen. 2:7. God did not just speak words, He *formed* man and then He *breathed His own breath* into man's nostrils. This tells us that man, more than anything else in God's creation, has the personal touch of God upon him.

Some people say that we are just animals who are smarter than the other animals. But according to Genesis, we are not just animals. There is nothing else in all of creation that Scripture says was created in God's image. We have a spirit placed inside of us by God that desires relationship with our Creator. Like Him, we think, we reason, we feel emotion, we create, we use our will to make choices, and we talk to each other and to God. Life is from God and it is very precious. This explains why we are torn inside by a deep grief when someone close to us dies. And it gives us a little understanding of why God was willing to give His own Son so that we could live forever with Him. Our Creator places great value upon us.

---

6. Notice in 1:26 God says, *"Let us make man in our image, in our likeness..."* Who do you think God was talking to? Explain your own thoughts, then read the section below.

Who was God talking to?

The writer of Genesis does not answer that question. He simply reports what God revealed to him--that God said, "Let *us* make man in *our* image." But there is a very interesting passage in the New Testament that can help us understand this. John, one of Jesus' closest disciples, explains several things clearly about the "Word of God" in his gospel.

Read John 1:1-5. What do these verses explain about the Word? In your own words, how would you express verses 1-3? (To understand clearly that the "Word" is Jesus, you will need to also read verses 14-18.)

---

7. Now return to Genesis 2 and read again verses 1-3. What did God do on the seventh day?

    Isaiah 40:28 tells us that God never gets tired. So, why do you think He rested on the seventh day?

    Do you think that a day of rest each week is important for people today?

8. Genesis 1 and 2 speak of God's abundant blessings upon the man and the woman. Here are a few of those blessings:

- God provides abundant food. (Genesis 1:29)
- God gives them purpose and meaningful work. (1:28 and 2:15)
- God gives the woman to the man as a friend and helper. (2:18 – 24)
- God creates them with child-like innocence; they are naked before each other and feel no shame. (2:25)
- Most importantly, the man and woman have a relationship with God. He talks with them, takes care of them, and wants the best for them. (1:28-29 & 3:8-9)

Before sin came into the world, life was simple, happy, and full of God's blessings. Look again at the 5 points above. Why is this picture of an innocent, sin-free world so beautiful to us today? Discuss your thoughts with the group.

What about evolution?

As you study Genesis, many questions may come to your mind about how the world was created. There are many things that these two chapters do not tell us, so we should be careful not to try to make Genesis a science book that is expected to explain every detail. But science cannot answer all the questions about the earth's beginnings either. Many scientists today are questioning Darwin's evolution theory. They see it as an inadequate explanation for the formation of life on earth. Perhaps you have been taught by atheists that everything in the world evolved by itself without a creator. Don't be afraid to believe what your common sense tells you. The universe has evidence of a Creator everywhere. Take a few minutes to discuss some of the evidence you see when you look at the world around you and at the heavens above. Don't forget to talk about the amazing design of your own body—your hands, your mind, your eyes!

---

9. Although the Bible does not tell us everything about how the world was created, there are several important things the writer of Genesis is trying to tell us in Chapters 1 and 2:

- **Everything was created by God**
- **He created it all very good**
- **He created us in His image**

As we begin this study of Genesis, it's important for us to see not only an all-powerful God but also a very loving Creator who cares about his creation. We will see much more of this as we continue through the following chapters of Genesis.

What does this mean for us today?
Application and Prayer

Read Psalm 100:3 several times.

1) How much do you think about the fact that the Creator of the universe has also made you, and that you are His?

Read Psalm 139:13-18.

2) How should it change our attitudes and actions each day if we always remember that our Creator has a beautiful plan for all of His creation?

3) Take a few minutes to worship our great Creator. Thank Him for His care of you.

Before the next study, read all of Genesis chapter 3.

2. THE FALL OF MAN INTO SIN
Genesis 3

Opening Question:

From the last study, what do you remember about how God created the world? How was the creation of man different from the creation of all the other creatures?

Introduction:

In our last study we saw that God created a beautiful and perfect world. But when we look at the world today we see many things that are not good—sickness and death; hatred and violence; envy, anger, and bitterness. What happened? This study will look at how sin first entered into God's creation. Before we begin the study of chapter 3, let's look back at a few verses of chapter 2 to help us understand what happened.

Read Genesis 2:8-9 and 15-17.

1. Look closely at verse 9. What were the names of the two special trees that God placed in the middle of the garden?

2. In verses 16-17, what did the Lord tell the man that he could eat? What did the Lord forbid? What did He say would happen if the man disobeyed and ate the fruit?

   Notice that the Lord blesses Adam and Eve with perhaps thousands of trees from which they can eat and enjoy his kindness to them. How do we sometimes miss all the beautiful blessings that God gives us in life by focusing on the one thing we cannot do?

Now let's look at how sin destroys the beautiful picture.

Read all of Genesis chapter 3.

3. Look carefully at the craftiness of the serpent in how he tempts the woman:

   - What does he say that places a doubt in the woman's mind? (Verse 1)
   - God said they would die if they ate of the tree. Does the serpent agree with God that there will be terrible consequences if she disobeys? (Verse 4)
   - How does the serpent place a seed of doubt in the woman's mind about God's loving care for her and Adam? (Verse 5)

Is the way the devil tempts us to sin similar to the way he tempted Eve? How? (Look at verses 1 and 4-5 again to answer this question.)

4. Let's look at the results of Adam and Eve's sin. Read each of the following verses:
   - **Verse 7: shame**
   - **Verses 8 & 9: hiding from God and fear of His presence**
   - **Verses 12 & 13: blaming someone else**

   Have you experienced these things? Explain how all of us experience the above consequences when we sin.

5. Genesis 1 and 2 speak of abundant beauty, peace and blessings in God's creation. Name all the curses that are described in chapter 3, verses 14-19.

6. There is one more curse. Read Genesis 3:22-24. Adam and Eve are banned from the tree of life. Even though they didn't immediately die physically, their spiritual death occurred that day. Their intimate communion with God was cut off. They were spiritually lost. How is this the worst of the curses?

How does the first sin affect you and me today?

It will be hard for us to see the effect of Adam's sin on us if we don't see ourselves as sinners and separated from God. In the New Testament, the apostle Paul helps us understand this in his letter to the Romans. Please take time now to read **Romans 5:12-19**.

Spiritual death and physical death began with Adam and continued in the human race as all participated in sin. If we don't realize that we are lost through Adam, then we won't see our need for Christ. Jesus' death for us on the cross will have no meaning. Romans 5 shows us the truth that because we are all Adam's offspring, we have all inherited his sinful, fallen nature.

We need a second birth—a spiritual birth. We must be born into Christ to escape the curse that came through the first man, Adam.

---

7. The Bible is full of prophecies. The very first prophecy in the Bible is found in Genesis 3. It is a prophecy spoken by God to the

serpent about something that will happen in the future. It is a mysterious prophecy. It tells the serpent of his future destruction.

Read Genesis 3:15. Who will crush the serpent? What do you think this means?

8. Even though God banned Adam and Eve from eating from the tree of life, He didn't abandon them. Nor did he destroy them. He still cared for them. Notice that he provided clothes for them since they now were filled with shame. How did God provide clothes for them? (Verse 21)

Why did God kill animals to cover Adam and Eve?

It is important to notice that animals were killed to cover Adam and Eve's shame. This is the first animal sacrifice in history. The sacrifice is made because of sin. Notice that Adam and Eve did not provide the sacrifice. In their sin and shame, fear taught them to hide from God. But God Himself provided the sacrifice for them. He covered the shame of their sin.

The fact that God provided a sacrifice to cover Adam and Eve's shame is a very important concept in the history and meaning of salvation. In the New Testament the writer of Hebrews says: **"...without the shedding of blood there is no forgiveness of sins." (Hebrews 9:22, ESV)** This important theme is covered throughout the Old and New Testaments. In the New Testament, we see that Jesus sheds His blood to forever cover the shame of all mankind.

Now let's look at something that the prophet Jeremiah said thousands of years after Adam and Eve. He was thinking deeply about the sinfulness of mankind. The sin in the garden had grown and filled the earth. But Jeremiah knew that sin was not just an outward action. Before Eve ate the fruit, she was deceived by the serpent. The desires of her heart became evil. Jeremiah knew that the hearts of all people had become filled with evil. He wrote despairingly: *"The heart is deceitful above all things and beyond cure. Who can understand it?" (Jeremiah 17:9)* Jeremiah knew his own heart was deceitful, too, and this verse shows that he was very discouraged when he looked within his own heart.

A few verses later (Jeremiah 17:14), he says: *"Heal me, O LORD, and I will be healed; save me and I will be saved, for you are the One I praise."*

Jeremiah knew that he must look outside himself to God, his only hope for salvation. He knew that if God brought healing and salvation then all would be well. His faith looked to God alone.

What does this mean for us today?
Application and Prayer

Read 1 John, chapter 1. (This is the first letter of John, not the gospel of John.)

1) In 1 John 1:7-9, John talks about walking in the light and confessing our sin. Explain how coming into God's light when we sin and confessing our sins to Him is different from the way Adam and Eve acted after they sinned. (See question 4 above)

2) Why is it important that all believers learn to walk in humility and trust in Jesus for forgiveness when they know they have committed sin?

3) End this study in prayer that the Lord would help you and the believers you meet with to be people who walk in the light. Quietly, in your heart, confess to Jesus anything that is keeping you from fellowship with Him. Thank and praise Him that He completely takes away your sin and makes you clean in His sight.

Before the next study, read all of Genesis chapters 4-10.

If you read one chapter each day, you can read all of this in one week. If you are unable to read all of this, at least read Genesis 4:1-12, skim all of chapter 5 but read at least 5:1-5 and 5:21-24, (You will find it interesting to see how long people lived in those days!) read all of chapters 6 and 7, and read chapter 9:7-17.

3. Sin Increases on the Earth
Genesis 4-10

Opening Questions:

Briefly review the events of Genesis 1-3. What details do you remember about how God created the world?

How did the disobedience of the woman and the man spoil God's wonderful creation? What did God do to provide covering for their bodies? How was this a symbol of what He would do to cover the sin and shame of all mankind?

Introduction:

Our first study showed the beauty of God's creation. Man and woman were created in God's image. But their fall into sin brought shame and curses upon them. They were sent away from the tree of life. In this study we will look at how sin in these two people began to affect all of their offspring.

Read Genesis 4:1-12.

1. In verses 6-7, what warning does God give to Cain?

    What happened because Cain did not listen to the warning? (Verse 8)

    Why is it important that we pay attention when God's Spirit speaks to us about wrong attitudes in our hearts?

2. What question does God ask Cain in verse 9?

    What is Cain's response to God?

    What do you think the answer is to Cain's question in verse 9? Are we our brother's keeper?

    What does society become like when people don't care for the needs of others?

Read Genesis 5:1-5 and verses 21-24 and verse 32.

3. Genesis 5 gives us an account of the generations from Adam to Noah and his sons. What 3 important things about the creation of man do you see in verses 1-2?

Did Adam and Eve really exist?

Some people say that Adam and Eve were just mythological people. In Genesis 5 we see that Adam and Eve were real people with real descendants on this earth. Adam had other sons and daughters, but the writer of Genesis is very careful here to show us that Adam's son Seth is the line that brings us to Noah. Other passages in the Old and New Testaments continue this line all the way to Jesus Christ, going through Abraham and David. (For examples, see Genesis 11:10-26, Matthew 1:1-17, and Luke 3:23-37.) Mythological people don't have descendants that connect with our real world. Genesis helps us to understand the true story of how man began and how sin began.

---

4. Look at Genesis 5:22-24. All the verses that talk about the other men end with "and he died." Notice that Enoch's story ends very differently from all the other stories.

   What do you think it means when it says that *"Enoch walked with God, and he was not, for God took him"*? (Verse 24, ESV)

   Think about your own life. Do you desire to walk more closely with God? Explain your desires.

Read Genesis 6:5-8.

5. The wickedness of man is increasing. What does verse 5 say about the thoughts of man?

   When people in society think about evil "continually" as verse 5 says, will the society be a stable and peaceful place? Explain your answer.

6. Read verse 6 again. This is the first time in the Bible that we read about God's emotional response to man's wickedness. In the past, did you ever think of God as one who grieves over the sin in this world? Explain your thoughts.

Where did sin come from?

In our study of Genesis 3 we saw that sin had a beginning. God did not create sinful people. He gave freedom to Adam and Eve—freedom to love God and follow Him. But this also meant that they were free to disobey Him. In the beginning they were like happy, innocent children.

The world was beautiful when they followed God's loving guidance. When they chose to disobey God, it didn't just affect them—the whole world became increasingly filled with violent and wicked adults who used their freedom to serve themselves rather than serving God and others. Thus we see that sin's entrance into the world can be traced all the way back to Adam and Eve.

Read Genesis 6:9-22.

7. Look again at verses 8-9. Why did Noah find favor with God?

8. Besides the animals, who went into the ark with Noah? (Verse 18) Describe briefly some of the preparations that God tells Noah to make?

Read Genesis 7:1-12.

9. For how many days did the rain fall on the earth? (Verses 4 & 12)

Read Genesis 7:22-24.

10. What happened to every living thing on the face of the earth?

11. After many years of building the ark, describe how you think Noah and his family must feel as they look out and see the waters covering the whole earth, while they are safe inside the ark.

If God is love, why did He destroy the people of Noah's day?

Here in the flood story, God makes a radical decision to destroy the whole world except for one man and his family. Some may ask the question: Why did God destroy all those people?

Look at Genesis 6:5 again. In Noah's days, the world needed judgment. It was destroying itself! God should not be seen as unloving when he judges the world. Instead we should be encouraged that God responsibly rules the world. The Bible continually calls God a righteous judge. (See Psalm 94:1-15.) His decisions are right and good. When an earthly judge condemns a mass murderer to life in prison, society rejoices because they know he will be prevented from continuing his murders. All people know that courts on earth have a responsibility to judge rightly. How much more do we expect God, who created the world with a glorious plan, to make judgments that condemn evil in this world. Throughout the entire Bible we learn that God judges the world righteously, even if sometimes

His judgments seem slow to us.

God's judgment of evil in the world is right. But He also teaches us that He will save people from His judgment if they follow His way of escape.

Finally the rain stops and the ground begins to dry. After a little more than a year in the ark, Noah and his sons and daughters-in-law come out. Noah builds an altar and offers some of the clean animals as a sacrifice of thanksgiving to God for keeping them safe. God gives Noah the same command that He gave to Adam and Eve in the beginning: they are to multiply and fill the whole earth. God then makes a covenant with Noah that He will never again destroy the entire earth by a flood. The rainbow is the sign of this promise. (Genesis chapters 9:1-17)

If you have not read all of the story of Noah and his family in chapters 6-9, it would be good to do that later on your own.

Quickly look over the list of Noah's descendants in Genesis 10.

12. In Genesis 5 we saw the generations from Adam to Noah. Genesis 10 tells us of the descendants of Noah from his 3 sons. What are those sons' names? (Verse 1)

    From these sons' descendants, what began to develop on the earth? (Verse 32)

Here we see the beginnings of early nations. We all come from Noah's descendants, though none of us know which line we come from. But from Genesis we gain some helpful information about our ancient history. Most importantly, we learn that God was there in all of this development. History back then was being directed by God, just as it is today. The following studies will help us see this more clearly.

What does this mean for us today?
Application and Prayer
Read 2 Peter 3:3-14.

In the New Testament, thousands of years after Noah, the apostle Peter talks about the final judgment of the world. He says that it will take people by surprise, just as the flood did in Noah's day.

1) Because judgment of this world will come like a thief and there will be no escape, what does Peter call followers of Jesus to do? (Read again verses 11-14.)

2) Why is it easy to be conformed to the world when ungodliness grows all around us?

Read 2 Peter 3:17-18.

3) Explain what you think verses 17-18 mean for you and the believers whom you meet with?

4) End this time in prayer that you may be people who are ready for the second coming of Jesus.

Before the next study, read all of Genesis chapter 11.

4. THE TOWER OF BABEL
Genesis 11

Opening Questions:

Briefly recall how sin began to affect mankind after Adam and Eve disobeyed God. What judgment did God finally bring on the earth? How was this judgment just? Why were Noah and his family spared?

Introduction:

In today's study we will look at what happened in a place called Babel. While sin always takes place in the heart and actions of individuals, sometimes an entire community joins together for sinful purposes. The story of Babel shows us how pride can grow in a community of people as a whole.

Read Genesis 11:1-9.

1. Look at verse 4 again. The people are uniting around a common goal. What is that common goal?

   In their conversation with each other, are the people wanting to unite together under God's leadership? Are they even thinking about God? Are they desiring to know what God might want for them as a society?

   Do you see any human pride in verse 4? Explain your thoughts.

What was the Tower of Babel?

The tower they were building may have been a "ziggurat." Many ruins of ziggurats have been found by modern archaeologists in the area of ancient Mesopotamia. Such towers were supposed to connect earth (men) to heaven (the gods) Verse 4 says, *"a tower that reaches to the heavens."* As people drifted further away from God, they tried to reach out to the "gods" that they had created in their minds.

Archaeologists tell us that the ziggurat towers were built to invite the gods to come down to their cities to bless them. They built a room at the top of the tower for the gods to come into, with a stairway that went down the tower. The pagan priests left food for the gods in the upper room, so that they would gain strength before they came down the stairs. The text in this story doesn't tell us for sure, but this story could be the beginning of the growth of idolatry, the worship of many gods. People were losing the knowledge that Adam and Eve once had of the true God.

Perhaps the pagan religions were beginning to develop at this time.

---

2. Read verse 4 again. Do you remember God's command to Adam and Eve: *"Fill the earth..."*? (Genesis 1:28) After the flood, God repeated the command to Noah and his family. (Genesis 9:1) What did the people say in Genesis 11:4 that disagrees with what God wanted?

3. The Bible doesn't tell us why the Lord told Adam and then Noah that they were to fill the earth. Why do you think God wanted men to be spread throughout the whole earth?

4. Read again verse 5. The people had said before that their tower was going to *"reach to the heavens."* How does verse 5 describe God's action? Did the tower actually reach heaven?

There is some humor in this story. The people want to make a name for themselves, so they build a tower that will reach the heavens, perhaps hoping to reach the gods. But God "goes down" to see it! The humans who are small think their tower is huge. However, it is a very, very small tower to God who created the universe! These humans have imagined themselves to be very important, but their pride has blinded them from seeing that they are not gods. And they will not reach the true God in their own strength. Their religious efforts to reach God prove to be empty and meaningless.

5. Read verses 6 and 7 again. The people were unified in this task. We usually think that when people are united, it is a good thing. Was the Lord pleased with their unity?

   Can you think of times when the unity of men can go against what God wants in the world?

Is unity always a good thing?

It is good for people to unite when their purposes are right and guided by God's wisdom and love. When people unite for purposes that ignore God or His word (as we see at Babel), the results can be very dangerous. We see from verse 4 that their unity was based on pride (*"let's make a name for ourselves"*) and fear (*"so we will not be scattered over the face of the whole earth"*). The Bible teaches that neither fear nor pride should be our guide in life. In fact, if we follow either motivation, dangerous results can happen to ourselves and others in this world.

In the 1930's and 40's, a man named Hitler brought together a society of people to make a name for themselves. Terrible destruction came to much of Europe and to many people before he was stopped. This has happened repeatedly throughout history as sinful men join together to build their own kingdoms, while ignoring God's way of doing things. All such societies sooner or later fall.

The prophet Isaiah described our situation in this way: *"We all, like sheep, have gone astray. Each of us has turned to his own way." (Isaiah 53:6)* The earth is full of individuals who have all gone their own way. The result is an unhealthy society. Over time the society disintegrates. Man, without God, cannot hold his world together.

---

6. Read verses 8-9. What two things happened when God confused their language?

    Babel means "confusion." Their unity is broken because they cannot talk to one another.

What was God's purpose in separating the people?

Some believe this was God's way of slowing down the rapid spread of sin in society. By God's hand, different cultures and language groups developed. People began to spread out around the world. God judged their sin by scattering them and making it impossible for them to accomplish their prideful goal. At the same time, He was accomplishing His purposes for men to spread out on the earth. In the book of Acts in the New Testament, the Apostle Paul spoke to the Athenians. He wanted them to see that there was only one God, and that He was in control of the world. He told them:

"From one man he made every nation of men, that they should inhabit the whole earth; and he determined the times set for them and the exact places where they should live. God did this so that men would seek him and perhaps reach out for him and find him, though he is not far from each one of us." (Acts 17:26&27)

Read Genesis 11:27-32.

7. In these verses we are introduced to Abram (later called Abraham) and Sarai (later called Sarah). From what city did they leave? (Verse 31) To what land were they going? (Verse 31)

    At the end of chapter 11, the writer turns our attention to something new that God begins to do. (Verses 27-32) At Babel we see that man's efforts leave him in confusion. Our next study will begin in Chapter 12. Here we will see God begin to unfold his amazing plan to save the whole world from the curses it has brought upon itself. This plan will bring blessing to the world through Abraham, a man of faith.

What does this mean for us today?
Application and Prayer
Read Psalm 115:1.

1) The people of Babel wanted to *"make a name for themselves."* Look again at the verse above. What does this verse say about Whose name deserves honor and why He deserves it?

Read Philippians 2:1-11.

2) In these verses, how did Jesus display the opposite attitude from the people of Babel?

3) Think about your own attitudes. Are there areas of your life where you seek to be known by others? What about your church? Or your Christian organization? Do you want to "make a name for yourselves" among other believers and groups?

    Sometimes we want to be exalted and honored as a leader, or to be known as the "best" church or "most effective organization." How does this go against Paul's exhortation in verses 3-7?

4) Look again at verses 9-11. Who alone deserves all praise and glory?

    If you have sought honor for yourself, pray now and ask God's forgiveness. Then, take some time to honor Him as Lord of all.

Before the next study, read all of Genesis chapters 12-15. If you are not able to read all of this, be sure to at least read Genesis 12:1-9 and all of chapter 15.

5. ABRAHAM: GOD'S CALL AND COVENANT
Genesis 12-15

Opening Question:

From our last study, how did man in his pride seek to make a name for himself apart from God? How did God respond to this?

Introduction:

Abraham is called the Father of those who have faith. His story is told in Genesis 11:26 – Genesis 25:11. As we read the story of Abraham (at the beginning called Abram), we see that he was a man who had faults and weaknesses like all people. But we also see that he was a man who responded in faith when God spoke to him. In this study, we will look at a few of the major events in his life. As we study, let's consider how Abraham's faith can inspire us to live by faith, too.

Read Genesis 12:1-9.

1. In verse 1, what did God command Abram to do?

    Now look at verses 4 and 5. How old was Abram when he left? Who went with him?

    What do you think were some of the difficulties that Abram experienced when he left everything to follow God's guidance to a strange land?

2. Look closely at verses 2 and 3. Name the different ways that God was going to bless Abram.

3. God also told Abram that *he would be a blessing* and that *"all peoples on earth"* would be blessed through him. This is an amazing promise! Everyone wants to be blessed by God. What do you think it means to be a blessing to others?

    Have you ever hoped your life would be a blessing to others? Explain your thoughts.

What was it like for Abram to obey God?

Abram stepped out in faith to follow God's direction. We don't know how God spoke to Abram. Was it with an audible voice? Or was it a voice deep within his heart which Abram knew was the voice of God? The Holy Book does not make that clear. But what is clear is that Abram left the security of his own land and went to a distant, strange land where

God sent him. They spoke a different language and had different customs. Abram was learning to trust this God who was slowly revealing Himself to Abram.

Surely there were many unanswered questions in Abram's mind about leaving his land. There always are when we follow God. God doesn't tell us all the details when He tells us to follow Him. The important thing is that we trust Him and obey Him like Abram did. And we can be sure that, just as Abram believed and brought blessing to himself and others, we can do the same. But the blessings God promised did not come immediately. In fact, they weren't all fulfilled in Abram's lifetime.

---

4. If you have a map of Abram's journey (often found in the back of a Bible, or you can find Biblical maps on the internet), find Ur, Abram's homeland. (See Genesis 11:31.) Find Haran, the city they first settled in. Approximately how many kilometers did Abram travel to Haran?

   Now find Canaan, the land to which God sent Abram. (See Genesis 12:5-6.) Approximately how many kilometers did Abram travel from Haran to Canaan?

5. When Abram arrives in Canaan, what does God say to him? (Verse 7) How does Abram respond to God's promise?

Abram learns to worship

Notice that in verse 8 Abram builds another altar. He continues to build altars to God at various times in his life. Abram took time to worship God. In those days, worship was expressed by sacrificing an animal on an altar. It expressed devotion and trust. It is important for us to remember that much of the world had lost its knowledge of the one true God. Idol worship was very common in Abram's day. In the eyes of the people of Canaan, Abram's God is just another god like theirs. Abram himself is learning more every day about the one true God. His knowledge of God is based on what God reveals to him. As he trusts and obeys, God reveals more of Himself to Abram.

Years pass. During this time, Abram travels to Egypt to escape a famine in Canaan. There he lies to Pharaoh about his wife, Sarah. Later, back in Canaan, he separates from his nephew, Lot, who has traveled with him from his former home back in Ur. Lot chooses to live in the fertile valley, which is also where the sin-filled cities of Sodom and Gomorrah are located. This will cause some serious problems for Lot which we will look at later in Study 7.

Abram, growing older, has remained childless. Sarai is still barren. How can God's promise made to Abram in Genesis 12 be fulfilled? How can Abram's descendants become a great nation if Sarai has no children? Also, God has told Abram that He will give him the land of Canaan. (See Genesis 13:14-18.) But Abram is living a semi-nomadic lifestyle as a foreigner there. Abram's faith in the one true God and His faithfulness to His word is being tested. How will God fulfill His promises for a child and for the land? Abram continues to wait as he grows older and older. (Genesis 12:10 – Genesis 14)

Why do you think God is waiting so long? What do you think is happening in Abram's life as he waits?

Let's look now at the covenant God makes with Abram.

Read all of Genesis 15.

6. What does God tell Abram in v. 1?

    Read verses 2-5 again. How would you describe Abram's emotions in verses 2-3? How does the Lord respond to him in verses 4-5?

7. Read verse 6 again. What one thing was necessary for God to count Abram righteous?

8. Read Genesis 15:17-21. Verse 18 tells us that God made a covenant with Abram. Before you read the box below, discuss this question: How do you think God's covenants with man are different from earthly contracts between people?

What Does It Mean For God to Make a Covenant with People?

The word "covenant" is used many times in the Old and New Testaments. Here are a few things the Holy Book teaches us about God's covenants with people.

1) **The covenant is initiated by God.**

   When two people today enter into a contract with each other, they each help to decide what the contract will include. Both sides are equal partners. This is not the case in a covenant between God and man. God comes to man and calls him to enter into covenant with Him. The covenant involves a promise God is making. God steps into man's world and shows him his purposes and His promise to fulfill those purposes. In the covenants of the Bible, we see a loving God who is guiding history in a positive way. The covenants reveal to us the marvelous plans of God.

2) **The covenant is a bond of love.**

   It is a sign of a deeply personal relationship between God and those He is making a covenant with. God calls men to enter the covenant by trusting Him and following His good purposes. This personal relationship is very different from the fear relationship that people had with idols. In God's covenant with the Jewish people in later books of the Old Testament, He calls them His people. They respond by calling Him their God.

3) **God is always faithful to His part of the covenant, even when his people are not.**

   Throughout history, man has often gone into idolatry. His will is very weak. God makes it clear that He will always do what He has said He will do.

Abram believed God and obeyed. When we read his story, we see a man who is invited by God into a relationship with Him. In response, Abram trusts and obeys God, and a relationship develops between them.

God gave us this story about Abram that we might desire the same thing. We were all made for relationship with God. Abram's steps of faith in the one true God blessed the whole world by teaching us the way of faith. And through this faith the child of promise was born to him. From this child the nation of Israel came into being, and through Israel was born Jesus the Messiah, the Savior of the world. God's purpose in blessing Abram was to restore His blessing to the world that was cursed by sin. And believers in Jesus are also called to be a blessing to others, as they bring the life and hope of Jesus Christ to the world.

What does this mean for us today?
Application and Prayer

In Genesis 12: 2-3 God said, *"...I will bless you...and all peoples on earth will be blessed through you."* God's blessings came to Abram not because he was a perfect man, but because He believed God's promises to him. It is the same with us. **In Genesis 15:6 it tells us *"Abram believed the Lord, and he credited it to him as righteousness."*** Abram was a blessed man in many ways, but most importantly, he was blessed because God counted him righteous. As a result, he was called "a friend of God."(James 2:23)

Several thousand years after Abram, the apostle Paul compares Abram's faith with the faith of believers in Christ.

Read Romans 4:1-8 and 22-25.

1) How is forgiveness of sins and being counted righteous by God the greatest blessing we can receive in life?

2) Abram's faith was tested throughout the years of his life, and our faith is also tested to see if it is genuine. Do you sometimes find it hard to believe that through Christ your sins are completely forgiven and that *through faith alone* you are clothed with Christ's righteousness? If so, why do you think it is hard for you to believe this?

3) Romans 4:20 says that Abram *"grew strong in his faith."* How can you and believers whom you worship with grow stronger in faith?

   Pray for a vibrant faith in your own life so that you might walk in all the blessings of Jesus Christ. And pray that your life, like Abram's life, will be a blessing to others.

Before the next study, read all of Genesis chapters 16-21.
If you are not able to read all of it, at least read all of chapters 16 and 17; chapter 18:1-15 and chapter 21:1-16.

All these people were still living by faith when they died.
They did not receive the things promised;
they only saw them and welcomed them from a distance.
And they admitted that they were aliens and strangers on earth.
People who say such things show that
they are looking for a country of their own.
If they had been thinking of the country they had left,
they would have had opportunity to return.
Instead, they were longing for a better country--a heavenly one.
Therefore God is not ashamed to be called their God,
for He has prepared a city for them.
Hebrews 11:13-16

6. ABRAHAM: THE BIRTH OF ISHMAEL & ISAAC
Genesis 16-21

Opening Questions:

From our last study, what two promises did God make to Abram? (Genesis 15:5 and 15:18) Although these promises seemed impossible, how did Abram respond to them? Why was Abram counted righteous before God?

Introduction:

In this study we will look at how God begins to fulfill his part of the covenant with Abram in a miraculous way. Abram and Sarai had to wait a long time to see that fulfillment. While they wait, they make a decision that still affects the world today.

Read Genesis 16.

1. Read again verses 1-4. What does Abram decide to do based on Sarai's suggestion? Who was Hagar? (verse 1)

Did Sarai and Abram do the right thing?

When the Lord spoke to Abram that he would have many descendants, he was married only to Sarai. Abram and Sarai have waited many years for the promise to be fulfilled through their union. Now they are very old and decide to make it happen in a way that they previously had not considered. Abram will try to have a child through Sarai's servant girl. Such things were not uncommon in those days, but it was not according to the way the Lord had spoken to them. At this point in the story, God does not comment on their action, but later in today's study we will see what God has to say about the matter. However, he still shows compassion towards Hagar.

What do you think about Sarai and Abram's decision?

2. When Sarai sends Hagar away because of conflict between them, what does God say about the son that will be born to Hagar? (verses 9-12)

Read Genesis 17:1-8.

3. Thirteen years have now passed since the birth of Ishmael. Abram is 99 years old and Sarai is 89. The Lord comes and speaks to him once again. God reminds Abram of His covenant with him.

What is Abram's part of the covenant that he is to keep? (See verse 1.) What do you think this means?

What is God's part of the covenant, that is, what three things does God promise to Abram? (Verses 2, 4, 7, & 8)

4. God then changes Abram's name to Abraham. Abram means "exalted father." Abraham means "father of a multitude." Why do you think God changed his name?

Read Genesis 17:9-11.

5. God tells Abram that he and future generations are to keep the covenant with him. What does God tell Abraham to do as a sign of this covenant? (verses 10-11)

Before you read the section below, if circumcision is a part of your culture, discuss its meaning to you and your people.

How important was circumcision among God's people in Bible times? How important is it today?

Genesis 17 is the first mention of circumcision in the Bible. God tells Abraham that it is a sign to show that they are keeping the covenant, a sign to show that they are followers of the one and only God. All males are required to do it. The one who will not do it has broken the covenant and is rejected by his people. Soon the circumcision ceremony was performed on all Jewish baby boys.

After Abraham, the Jewish people were not always faithful to keep the covenant, even when they kept the outward sign of circumcision. Often they worshiped other gods. Hundreds of years after Abraham, Moses challenged the people to not wander from God's ways and spoke to them of the real meaning of circumcision. They were to circumcise their stubborn hearts. (Deuteronomy 10:16)

Later in the New Testament, John the Baptist rebuked the people who came to him. He told them not to say, *"We have Abraham as our father" (Matt. 3:9).* In other words, "We are circumcised Jewish people, so God must accept us." John warned them that they were in spiritual danger. He called them to repent and follow God's ways wholeheartedly, not just with external signs like circumcision.

Before he met Jesus, the apostle Paul was a Jewish religious leader who believed strongly in the importance of circumcision. Later, as a follower of Jesus, he warned Christians that they should not look to circumcision to save them. This is the central teaching in Galatians. Paul summed up his words like this: *"For neither circumcision counts for anything, nor uncircumcision, but a new creation." (Galatians 6:15,ESV).* Paul was saying that being born again by the Spirit through faith in Jesus the Messiah is what marks believers as being God's people.

Today in some parts of the world, Christians circumcise their boys because they believe it is more sanitary and healthy. It is not, however, something Christian believers trust in for salvation.

Read Genesis 17:15-22.

6. How does Abraham respond to this news that Sarah will have a son? (See verses 17-18.) How old is Abraham? How old is Sarah? (Notice that her name has now also been changed.)

7. In these verses, God makes His promise to Abraham more clear. Through which son will God continue His covenant? (verses 20-21)

Read Genesis 18:1-15.

8. This event happens soon after God's promise made in the previous chapter. In verse 12, how does Sarah respond to the news the messenger brings?

9. Read again verses 13-14. What does he ask Abraham about Sarah? If you had been in Sarah's place, how do you think you would have responded?

Read Genesis 21:1-7.

10. Think about the messenger's question (18:14) and the fulfillment of the promise in these verses of Genesis 21. Remember that earlier they decided to have a child through Hagar. But God clearly stated that the child of promise would come through Sarah.

    Try to imagine and describe the emotions of Abraham and Sarah after all their years of waiting for the fulfillment of God's word.

Read Genesis 21:8-21.

11. Describe God's word to Abraham about Sarah's reaction to Ishmael. (verse 12-13)

Ishmael and Isaac

God promises blessing to both Ishmael and Isaac—both sons will become great nations. Ishmael became the father of the Arabic people. Isaac, however, is the special son of promise. From him will come the nation of Israel that God will have a special covenant relationship with. God will reveal Himself to Israel and they, in turn, are to be a testimony to all nations of the relationship God wants to have with all mankind. Finally, in God's timing, He will send the promised Redeemer through Isaac the child of promise.

What does this mean for us today?
Application and Prayer

Abraham and Sarah waited for many years for the promise of a child to be fulfilled. At one point in their waiting, they decided to make it happen in their own wisdom and in their own way with Hagar, Sarah's servant girl.

God shows them several things about Himself in this story. And He teaches these things to us again and again throughout the scriptures.

- First, God always keeps His promises. There is always a purpose for the way He does things and the time in which He chooses to do them, though we may not understand what He is doing.
- Second, nothing is impossible for Him. Sarah and Abraham thought that being old meant they would not be able to have a child. But God said He would do it, and He did it! Nevertheless, Abraham and Sarah had to wait on God and trust Him.

Read Proverbs 3:5-6 through several times.

1) Do you sometimes try to make things happen in your way when you know you must learn to wait on God?
2) How can you learn to do things His way and trust that He will bring about the right results in His timing?
3) Take time now to pray that the truths of the above proverb would be fulfilled in your own life.

Before the next study, read Genesis 18:16-31 and all of chapter 19.

7. THE DESTRUCTION OF SODOM AND GOMORRAH
Genesis 18:16-33 and 19:1-29

Opening Questions:

In our last study, we saw God fulfill a promise that He had made to Abraham. What was that promise? How old were Abraham and Sarah when it was fulfilled? What did God command Abraham to do to show that they were set apart as His chosen people?

Introduction:

In this study we will go back and look at a story that we skipped over in the last study. Genesis 12 tells us that when Abraham left the land of his ancestors in obedience to God, his nephew Lot went with him. Chapter 13 tells us how Abraham and Lot separated from each other. Lot moved into a fertile valley where there were also two cities, Sodom and Gomorrah. In this study we will look at God's judgment on those two cities and consider why He judged them so severely. This story begins right after the three men have visited Abraham and Sarah and told them they will have a son. Isaac has not yet been born.

Read Genesis 18:16-33.

1. Why does the Lord say He will reveal to Abraham what He is about to do? (See verses 17-19.)

   If Abraham understands that the destruction of Sodom and Gomorrah is clearly a judgment from God, how might this build in him a healthy fear of God? How might it encourage him to train his descendants to walk in God's ways?

2. Why is the Lord going to destroy Sodom and Gomorrah? (Verse 20)

3. Read again verses 23-25. What request does Abraham make of the Lord?

   In verse 25, how does Abraham appeal to God as a just judge?

   Does the Lord agree to do what he requests? (v. 26)

   How does knowing that God is loving and just encourage you to pray with confidence?

4. Notice Abraham's boldness as he continues to intercede on behalf of the city of Sodom. (Read again verses 27-32.)

How many righteous persons does the Lord finally agree are necessary in order to spare the city from destruction?

Read Genesis 19:1-29.

5. When the two men who have just left Abraham arrive at the gate of Sodom, who greets them and offers them hospitality? Who is Lot? (If you have forgotten, look back at the introduction to this study.)

6. Look back at verses 1-2. Why do you think Lot strongly insisted that the men not sleep in the square of the city?

7. Read again Genesis 18:20. After reading the actions of the men of Sodom in Genesis 19, explain why the Lord might say that the "outcry against Sodom and Gomorrah is so great and their sin so grievous...."

Lot's interaction with the men of Sodom

Lot's willingness to risk his own life to protect his guests is admirable. His willingness to sacrifice his two daughters for their sake, however, shows that he is not looking to God for help, nor is he caring about his daughters. Instead he is desperately trying to find a way out of a bad situation using his own wisdom. Thankfully, the angels come to his rescue and save both him and his daughters.

---

8. Read again verses 12-14. Why does the angel say that the city of Sodom is going to be destroyed? What must Lot and his relatives do? God's Word tells us that there is nothing hidden from Him. Have you ever thought that as the sins of a city reach the ears of God, they could lead to His judgment?

    What are some sins of today's cities that may grieve the Lord greatly?

9. According to verse 14, how do the men who are engaged to marry Lot's daughters respond to Lot's warning?

10. Read verses 15-22. Why do you think Lot hesitated? What do you think might have been holding him back?

11. How many people in all were rescued from Sodom? Remember Abraham's final request in Genesis 18:32. Were ten righteous persons found?

How does Lot respond to an evil society?

Read 2 Peter 2:7-8. In these verses the Apostle Peter tells us that Lot was greatly disturbed in his soul by the evil around him. He was a righteous man living in a very ungodly environment. We see from his treatment of the two angels who visit his city, that he is very different from the other men of the city. When he meets the visitors in the marketplace, he is concerned for their safety. He invites them in to his home and he offers hospitality to them. He risks his own life to protect them.

However, although Lot does not participate in the wickedness of those around him, he hesitates when he is warned to leave. He seems to have grown comfortable with his surroundings. The evil bothers him, but he doesn't want to separate himself from it.

How do you respond to the evil you see in the society around you today? Do you just accept it as the way things are? Or do you pray earnestly for the kingdom of God to come and change society? Are you willing to speak out against evil when necessary?

12. Read Genesis 19:23-29 again. How did God destroy the cities of Sodom and Gomorrah and the other villages of the plain? What do you think Lot must be thinking now?

13. How did Lot's wife disobey the angel's command? (Look back at verse 17.) What happened to her? (Verse 26)

    Many years later, Jesus spoke about the judgment on Sodom and Gomorrah when he talked about the judgment upon the world at the time of His return. He said in Luke 17:32-33, *"Remember Lot's wife! Whoever tries to keep their life will lose it, and whoever loses their life will preserve it."*

    What do you think Jesus meant by these words, which he connected to Lot's wife?

14. What do you think Abraham might have been thinking and feeling as he stood and looked out at the smoke rising above the plain below him? (Verses 27-28)

What does this mean for us today?
Application and Prayer

The darkness and wickedness of this world will not continue forever. The world, like Sodom and Gomorrah, is under judgment. We are called to leave Sodom and flee to Christ. We are also called to proclaim Him to a rebellious world. He is their only hope for escaping the judgment. Sinners are blinded from seeing the judgment coming. Some mock the message that danger is ahead and that sin will be judged.

Abraham showed God's heart of love for a sinful world when he prayed, even for the salvation of wicked Sodom. In a similar way, we who have received God's mercy for ourselves, begin to care for the lost world that we live in. We care for our family members who don't know him. We care for the people around us—our neighbors, the people we work with, the people of our city or village. We see judgment coming. How can we help them escape it?

Abraham spoke to God on behalf of the people of Sodom and Gomorrah, that they might be spared. Jesus died for all of lost humanity, and we are called to pray for them. We pray that people's eyes might be opened so that they come to Jesus. We pray for wisdom and power to help lead them out of darkness and into the light.

1) Think about the prayers that you pray for others. Who do you pray for and what do you pray for them?

Read 2 Peter 3:9.

2) Do you share in Christ's burden that none perish but that all come to repentance?

3) Throughout history believers have united to pray for their cities and nations, for awakenings and for the spread of the gospel. Many revivals and outpourings of God's Spirit have occurred because of the prayers of God's people.

    Do you ever pray for whole cities? For whole nations?

4) Do you want to grow in praying for others? Can you think of times and ways to gather with other believers to pray for this lost world?

    Ask God now to help you pray more for this world.

Before the next study, read all of Genesis chapters 22-25. If possible, take some time to meditate on chapter 22.

8. ABRAHAM IS TESTED; ABRAHAM'S DEATH
Genesis 22-25

Opening Questions:

In our last study, why did God destroy the cities of Sodom and Gomorrah? Who did God rescue? Why did God rescue them?

Explain how Abraham interceded for Sodom. Although the Lord agreed to Abraham's request, why did He not spare the city?

Introduction:

As we saw in Study 6, Abraham had two sons. Ishmael was born in the natural way through a slave woman. Isaac was the son of God's promise and was born in a supernatural way. God promised blessing to both Ishmael and Isaac, but He said that Isaac would be the one who would carry on His covenant promise. Now God asks Abraham to do something that seems to make that promise through Isaac impossible. Will Abraham trust God and obey what He tells him to do? In this study we will see how much Abraham's faith has grown.

Read Genesis 22.

1. Read verse 2 again. What did God ask Abraham to do? Look carefully at the verse. What does God say about Abraham's son, Isaac?

    How do you think Abraham felt toward his son Isaac? What do you think he might have been thinking about as he set out for the place that God would show him?

    Why did God ask Abraham to do this, according to verse 1?

2. Read verse 3. Did Abraham argue with God? How soon did Abraham set out to obey God's command?

    Think about your own obedience to God. God asked Abraham to do an extremely difficult thing, yet he trusted God and obeyed from his heart. What kind of obedience do you think pleases God?

3. Read verses 7-8 again. What question does Isaac ask his father in verse 7?

    Now read again Abraham's answer in verse 8. What do you think Abraham might have been thinking when he said this?

"God will provide for Himself the lamb..." (Gen. 22:8, ESV)

Here we see a beautiful picture of how much Abraham's faith in God has grown. God has not told Abraham what He is going to do. Abraham has no evidence that God will provide the lamb for the offering. Nevertheless, he trusts that God will fulfill His promise to bring forth a great nation from Isaac's offspring. Abraham's words are also prophetic, looking forward to the time when God will once again provide the Lamb for the offering. (See John 1:29.) But when God provides the Lamb in the form of His own Son given for the sin of the world, there is no substitute.

---

4. Now read again the rest of the story in verses 9-19. Look again at verses 9-10. What does Abraham do in these verses? How close does he come to actually sacrificing his son?

   What do you think Abraham must have been feeling as he raised the knife?

5. Read again verses 11-12. Look closely at what the Lord says to Abraham in verse 12. What does Abraham's offering of his son show?

   Explain your thoughts of what it means to "fear God."

   How can Abraham be called "a friend of God" on one hand (see James 2:23) and "fear God" on the other hand? Is it possible to fear God and love Him at the same time? Explain your thoughts.

6. How does God provide the animal for the sacrifice? (Verse 13) What do you think Abraham must be thinking and feeling now?

Why would God ask Abraham to sacrifice his son?

Many years after Abraham, the people began to disobey God and offer their children as burnt offerings to the false god Molech. In Jeremiah 32:35 God makes it very clear how he feels about child sacrifice. (See also Deuteronomy 18:10.) In Genesis 22:1 it says that this was a test. God's plan from the beginning was that He would provide for the sacrifice. But He is testing Abraham to see what is in his heart. Which does Abraham love more—his son Isaac, or God? In verse 12 we see that Abraham passed the test. He obeyed God, even at the cost of his son.

7. Discuss some of the ways this story is a picture of what God will do in the New Testament in giving His Son for us.

   Does this story about Abraham make that story in the New Testament more meaningful to you? Explain your thoughts.

8. God repeats His promise to Abraham in verses 15-18. What promises does He once again make? How does Abraham's obedience affect all people? (Verse 18)

After this, Sarah dies at 127 years of age. Then we have the beautiful story of how God provides a wife for Isaac in Genesis 24. If you haven't read this yet, be sure you take time to read it on your own. In chapter 25, Abraham takes another wife and has other children. Then he dies at the age of 175. In the next study we will see how God continues to work through Abraham's descendants to fulfill His purposes.

What does this mean for us today?
Application and Prayer

In the mid 1900's a young mother who was a missionary in India walked up a mountain in northern India. She was taking her 7-year-old daughter to a boarding school where she would live and study for nine months each year. At the time, this was the little girl's only option for an education. As they walked, the mother wept bitter tears. "How can I leave my little girl so far away from her family? How can I give her up?" Then the Lord reminded her in her heart of Abraham's words to his servant as he went away to offer Isaac as a sacrifice: *"I and the boy will go over there and worship." (Genesis 22:5 ESV)* Just like Abraham's offering of his son, her giving up her little daughter for the sake of serving God was an act of worship, a gift that she could give to show her love for God. In her heart, she offered up her child to God. Suddenly, she was filled with joy and peace. Years later, that same daughter returned to also serve God as a missionary in India.

In this study, God tests Abraham and Abraham proves by his actions that he loves God even more than he loves his own son. In the book of Matthew in the New Testament, Jesus calls His followers to have that same kind of love for Him.

Read Matthew 10:37-39.

1) In verse 37, what does Jesus say about the person who loves father or mother or son or daughter more than Him?

2) Think about the members of your family who are closest to you, the people whom you love the most. What if God asked you to leave them to spread the Good News? Would you say "yes" to Him?

What if He asked you to give your blessing to a close family member who felt called by God to a dangerous place? Could you do that?

3) Read the passage of scripture from Matthew again. Do you believe that verse 39 is really true?

4) Take some time now to talk to God about these verses. Ask Him to help you to commit your whole life and the lives of those you love to serve Him in any way He desires.

Before the next study, read Genesis 25:19-34 and chapters 27-28.

Although we will not discuss chapter 26, it would be good to read that also. (See page 75)

9. Jacob: Chosen and Blessed by God
Part 1, Genesis 25-28

Opening Questions:

From our last study, how did God test Abraham? Why did He test him? How was this a picture of what God would do for all people through Jesus?

Introduction:

As we read through Genesis, we see that God continues to reveal who He is and what His purposes are for His creation. In Genesis 26, two times God repeats to Isaac the promise that He has made to Abraham to make him a great nation and to give him the land of Canaan. Like his father Abraham, Isaac builds an altar and worships God. This study and the next one will look closer at some of the significant events in the life of Isaac's sons, and especially in the life of Jacob.

Read Genesis 25:21-34.

1. Twenty years after their marriage, Isaac's wife Rebekah becomes pregnant with twins. Read again verses 22-23. What does the Lord tell Rebekah about the two sons who will be born to her?

2. In your own words, tell briefly what happens in verses 27-34. What did Esau trade for a dish of food? How did Esau feel about what he traded? (Verse 34.)

3. In this story, we see a little of the characters of the two brothers. What kind of person do you think Jacob is?

What does Jacob's name mean?

"Jacob" means "person who grasps the heel," which also means "deceiver." As we study Jacob's story, it becomes clear that Jacob's name describes his character. We have just read about the first time that Jacob takes advantage of someone else. In Genesis 27 we will see that he cheats his brother again in an even bigger and more important matter.

Read Genesis 27:1-4.

4. What does Isaac ask Esau to do? What is Isaac preparing to do before he dies? (Verse 4)

What was the blessing that Isaac was about to give?

The blessing that Isaac was preparing to give to his son Esau was very important in the culture of that day. It established the firstborn son as the new head of the family. In this case it also included the promises of God to Abraham to make his offspring a great nation and to give them the land of Canaan. In Genesis 27:5-17 we learn that Rebekah has overheard Isaac's request of Esau, and she convinces Jacob to deceive his father into giving the blessing to him (Jacob) rather than to his brother. The blessing rightfully should have belonged to Esau as the oldest, but God had said before the boys were born that the older would serve the younger. At this time in his life, Jacob does not seem like a very good choice to carry on God's promised blessing to all peoples on earth. As we continue to study Jacob's life, we will see how God will work through many circumstances to teach him His ways.

Read Genesis 27:18-41.

5. In your own words, briefly describe the blessing that Isaac gave to Jacob. (Verses 28-29)

6. When Esau sold his birthright (that is, his right to a greater inheritance as the firstborn son) for a bowl of food, he did not feel badly about it. This time it is different.

   Look again at verses 34 and 41. How did Esau respond this time to his brother's deception?

With Rebekah's help, Jacob is sent away to his uncle Laban's. On the way, God speaks to him one night through a dream. This is the first time we read of God speaking to Jacob.

Read Genesis 28:10-22.

7. Describe what Jacob saw in his dream. Read again verses 13-15. What does God say to Jacob?

Notice that God is repeating to Jacob the promises that He has made to his father Isaac and his grandfather Abraham. None of these have yet seen the promises fulfilled; the family is still few in number, and they are foreigners and nomads in the land they have been promised. But God is looking for faith. Will they believe Him, even without seeing evidence?

8. How does Jacob respond to God's promise? (See verses 16-22.)

9. Why do you think Jacob is afraid? (Verse 17) What does Jacob want to see happen before he personally makes the Lord to be his God? (verse 20-21).

God reveals Himself to Jacob

Let's remember that in the land of Canaan where Jacob lives, the people are pagan worshipers of false gods. Jacob himself does not know the Lord, except by the stories he has heard from his father and grandfather. The Lord spoke a number of times to Abraham and Isaac. Now the Lord chooses a critical moment in Jacob's life to appear to him. He has left his father's home and is going to a strange land. He is probably filled with anxiety.

Jacob thinks he is alone, but in the darkness of night, he sees the angels of God and the Lord speaks to him from heaven. In the dream, Jacob is confronted with the fact that God is real, and that He is with Jacob. The Lord speaks to Jacob the same great promises that He has made to Abraham and Isaac. But Jacob's response is conditional. He says that if the Lord will do certain things, then Jacob will call Him his God. Jacob recognizes that God is with him and has spoken to him, but he is not yet ready to fully put his trust in the God of his fathers. It will take many years and many trials before he is ready to fully submit to God.

What does this mean for us today?
Application and Prayer

Jacob's father Isaac and his grandfather Abraham were men of faith. Genesis 15:6 tells us that Abraham was counted righteous before God because he believed God's promises to him, even though many years passed before the promises were fulfilled. This was Jacob's spiritual heritage. Jacob, however, wants to see proof of God's faithfulness before he fully believes.

As you read the verses below, think about your own faith. Are you more like Abraham, or are you more like Jacob?

Read Hebrews 11:1 and 11:6 several times.

In these verses the writer gives us a definition of faith.

1) In your own words, tell what you think it means to have faith in God's word and in His promises.

2) What are some promises from God's Word that He has made to all of His followers? Do you have a promise from His Word that you hold onto in difficult times? If so, tell the group about it.

3) How would you like to see your faith grow in the weeks ahead?

Take some time now to talk to God about this.

Before the next study, read Genesis 29-36.

If you are not able to read all of this, at least read chapter 29:14-30, chapter 30:25-43, chapter 31:1-13, chapter 32:1-12 and 22-32, and all of chapter 33.

10. JACOB: CHOSEN AND BLESSED BY GOD
Part 2, Genesis 29-35

Opening Questions:

From our last study, tell briefly the two situations where Jacob cheated his brother. Why did Jacob have to flee to his uncle's home? Describe the dream that Jacob had while on the way. What promises did God make to Jacob? What did Jacob promise God?

Introduction:

Jacob now arrives at his Uncle Laban's home and is greeted warmly. But it is there that he will become the victim of his uncle's dishonesty. God will allow him to experience some of the same kind of treatment that he has given to his brother.

Read Genesis 29:14-30.

1. Describe how Jacob is cheated in these verses. Why does Laban say he could not give him Rachel first? (Verse 26)
2. How many years in total did Jacob work for Rachel? What does verse 20 say about his love for her?

Genesis 29:31-30:34 tells about the birth of Jacob's children (except for Benjamin, who was born later). On your own you can read this story of the competition between the two wives and their two handmaidens, who were also given to Jacob as wives. Finally Jacob decides it's time to return home. At this time, he is cheated once again by Laban.

Read Genesis 30:25-36.

3. How has God blessed Laban because of Jacob? (Verses 27 and 29-30)
4. Describe briefly how Laban cheats Jacob in verses 32-36.
5. In the past, Jacob has always gotten what he wanted, but now the cheater himself is cheated. How do you think he must feel?

   What do you think might be happening to Jacob's pride?

Jacob continues to work for Laban. God blesses him with sheep and goats in spite of Laban's dishonesty. (Genesis 30:37-43) After 20 years of working for his uncle, God speaks to Jacob and tells him that it's time to return to his father's home. In chapter 31 you can read on your own about how he fled from Laban with his wives, children, servants, and large flocks and herds of animals. On the way to his father's home, he hears that his brother Esau is approaching.

Read Genesis 32:3-12.

6. How does Jacob respond to the news that Esau is coming to meet him? (Verse 7)

7. Twenty years have now passed since Jacob stole his brother's blessing and had to flee from his father's house. At that time it seems that Jacob was the one who was in control over his brother. Read again verses 4-5. What change in attitude do you see in Jacob's message to his brother?

8. Now read again Jacob's prayer to God. (Verses 9-12) What do you see in this prayer that shows you that Jacob has been humbled? (Look especially at verse 10.)

    What promises does Jacob remind God of? (Verses 9 and 12)

Jacob sends numerous gifts ahead of him to his brother. As he waits nervously for them to meet, during the night, Jacob has a very unusual experience with God.

Read Genesis 32:22-32.

9. Describe Jacob's encounter with the man, whom he later recognizes as the Lord. (Verse 30) What did the man do to Jacob? (Verse 25) How might this have further humbled Jacob?

10. What did Jacob demand from the man? (Verse 26) What new name did the man give to Jacob? Jacob's new name means, "one who struggles with God." Do you think this was an appropriate name for Jacob? Explain your answer.

Read all of Genesis 33.

11. Jacob knows that he does not deserve kindness from his brother. How does he approach Esau? (Verse 3) How does Esau respond? (Verse 4)

    Do you think that Esau has forgiven Jacob? Explain your thoughts.

After his meeting with Esau, God tells Jacob to go and camp at Bethel, the place where he had his first vision of God twenty years before.

Read Genesis 35:1-3 and 6-15.

12. Look back at Jacob's prayer to God the first time he came to Bethel when he was on his way to his uncle's home twenty years earlier. (Read Genesis 28:20-22.)

Now read again Genesis 35:3. Think back over all that has happened to Jacob in the past twenty years. How has God kept his promise to Jacob?

How does Jacob respond to God's faithfulness to him? (Verses 3 and 6-7)

13. What promise that He made to Jacob's fathers does God now repeat to Jacob? (Verses 11-12)

Notice that Jacob has just recently begun to build altars to worship God. This is another sign of how he has changed. God has been faithful to him and now, as he promised twenty years before, the God of his fathers is his God also.

What was the purpose of an altar?

In Genesis, Abraham, Isaac and Jacob all made altars. After them, the Israelites continued to make altars. But what were they? Altars were platforms often made of earth or stone. They made them for various reasons, but the foundational reason was to worship God and show their allegiance to Him as their God, and not to idols. Altars were also built to thank God for His promises, for His protection and for His provision. On the altar, sacrifices of animals were made (and often burned) with the smoke rising to God. Later in Exodus, God commanded that they offer animals as sacrifices for sin.

Why don't Christians build altars?

The writer of Hebrews tells us that *"we have an altar"* – but it is not like the altars of the Old Covenant. (Hebrews 13:10-15) Their animals were imperfect sacrifices. On the cross, however, God, not man, made the sacrifice. He offered His Son as the perfect sacrifice for us. He is *"the Lamb of God who takes away the sin of the world." (John 1:29)* It is always at this altar – the cross of Jesus – where believers worship. It is not a physical place, but rather a spiritual place in our hearts where we remember what God did for us. Our worship can take place anywhere— we don't need a physical altar or a special mountain or city. Wherever we are can be a holy place for worship. (See John 4:19-24). Through Jesus we offer thanks and praise to God for His amazing grace and love. And it is at the cross that we give our lives to Him again each day.

What does this mean for us today?
Application and Prayer

When we study the life of Jacob we see that God was always with him through the ups and downs of his life. God also was working to change him and make him a godly man.

In the New Testament the Apostle Paul spoke about this to the believers at Philippi.

Read Philippians 1:6.

1. Read this verse again slowly and take a few minutes to think about what it means.

    When you put your faith in Jesus as your Savior, He began to work in you to make you more like Himself. How have you seen God working in your life to change you since that time?

2. What would you like to see God change in you in the weeks and years ahead?

3. Take some time now to talk to Him about it.

Before the next study, read Genesis chapter 37 and chapter 39:1-6

11. Joseph: A Man of Faith and Forgiveness
Part 1, Genesis 37 & 39:1-6

Opening Questions:

From our previous study, why did Jacob leave his father's home to go to his uncle's? How did he change during the time that he was away? What promises that God had made to Abraham and Isaac did God repeat to Jacob? Tell about some of the ways that God revealed Himself to Jacob.

Introduction:

In this study we will look at the first part of the fascinating story of the life of Joseph, one of Jacob's twelve sons. Jacob, with his wives and children, along with his many flocks and herds, has returned to the land of his father. In this study and the next two, we will see how God continues to work out His good plan in some surprising ways.

Read Genesis 37:1-11.

1. Why did Joseph's brothers hate him? (There are two reasons given in verses 2-4.)

2. Describe the two dreams that Joseph had in verse 6 and verse 9. How did his brothers respond to these dreams? (verses 8, and 11) How did his father respond? (verse 10)

    How do you think you would have responded if you had been one of the brothers?

Jacob's family are nomads who live in tents and move around, pasturing large flocks of animals. One day Joseph's brothers are out taking care of the flocks far from home. Jacob sends Joseph to check on the brothers' well-being and the condition of the animals. (Genesis 37:12-17)

Read Genesis 37:18-24.

3. What do the brothers call Joseph? (Verse 19) Why do they call him that?

4. What do they decide to do to him? (Verse 20) What feelings do you think have been growing in their hearts toward Joseph?

    Who saves Joseph from being killed? What is his plan?

Read Genesis 37:25-36.

5. What do the brothers see in verse 25? Where is it going? Why? (Verse 25)

What do Joseph's brothers do with him? (Verses 27-28)

How do the brothers deceive their father? (Verses 31-33) How does he respond? (Verses 34-35) Imagine the grief that Jacob must be feeling.

6. What happens to Joseph in Egypt? (Verse 36)

7. When we read the events of Genesis 37, we see a family with many relational problems. Discuss in each point below how the wrong attitudes and actions of each family member contributed to this tragedy.

- Jacob's favoritism toward Joseph
- Joseph's immature actions toward his brothers
- The brothers' jealousy and hatred toward Joseph
- The brothers' deceptive scheme to hide their sin from their father
- How do similar attitudes and actions in families today destroy relationships?

Read Genesis 39:1-6.

8. Whose household is Joseph sold into? (Verse 1)

Why is Joseph so successful? (Verses 2-3)

Look at verses 3-6. Discuss Potiphar's response to Joseph's success. What position is Joseph given in Potiphar's house?

Let's think about Joseph's situation.

Discuss briefly how hard it must have been for Joseph to be taken from his father's house where he was the favorite, thrown into a well, and then sold as a slave in a foreign country far from home. Remember that he was only 17 years old at this time. What emotional pain do you think he was experiencing?

Do you think it would have been easy for him to serve his master faithfully every day and not sink into despair? How do we know that God was with him during this difficult time? Take a few minutes to discuss these questions.

---

9. Look again at verses 2-6. We are not told about Joseph's attitude toward his work or his master. From these verses, what kind of servant do you think Joseph must have been?

When we find ourselves in unjust and painful situations, why is it important that we continue to serve God and others faithfully?

What was Joseph's attitude?

Joseph became a slave because of the hate-filled actions of others. He had to choose how he would respond. When we read this part of his story we are not told anything about what he is thinking. Did he have thoughts of bitterness and anger against his brothers? Was he battling with depression or despair? Did he at times want to give up on life? We don't know. But if he did, he overcame these things. We will see later in his life that he holds no bitterness against his brothers.

What does this mean for us today?
Application and Prayer

Many years after Joseph, the Apostle Paul gave some advice to slaves. This advice is useful for any of us today who must work under the supervision of others. It is especially helpful if we work for someone who is difficult or unfair. It is also good advice for us in our family situations. If we have people over us in our home or family who are unjust and demanding, these verses can encourage us.

Read Ephesians 6:5-8.

1) According to verses 5, 6, & 7, how should the slave work for his master?

    Who should the slave think of as his real Master?

2) Think about your own life. In your home or in your workplace, do you do your work for God or only to please people?

    Do you do your work cheerfully, or do you often complain?

    Do you sometimes do extra work just to be helpful, or do you just do the minimum that you have to do?

3) How can it help you be a better servant of others to realize that God sees everything and will reward everyone for what they have done?

4) What do you think needs to change in your attitude toward your work or your situation in life? Take some time now to talk to God about it.

Before the next study, read Genesis chapters 39-41.

12. Joseph: A Man of Faith and Forgiveness
Part 2, Genesis 39:7-41:57

Opening Questions:

From our last study, why did Joseph's brothers hate him? What did they do to him? Who was he sold to in Egypt? How did God bless him in Egypt?

Introduction:

In spite of the fact that Joseph is a slave, he has a high and respected position. In this study we will see how quickly that changes in a way that is very unjust to Joseph. Yet Joseph will continue to be a man of integrity and to honor God with his life and his work.

Read Genesis 39:7-23

1. How does Potiphar's wife tempt Joseph? (Verses 7&10) How does Joseph respond to the temptation? (Verses 8-9)

"How then could I do such a wicked thing and sin against God?"
(Joseph to Potiphar's wife, Gen.39:9)

Joseph thought he was speaking only to Potiphar's wife. He did not know when he said this that we would be reading it thousands of years later. His actions teach us what the Bible calls **"the fear of the Lord."** The fear of the Lord does not mean that we are afraid of God so that we cannot come near to Him. Through Christ and His great love shown to us through the cross, we can come confidently into God's presence. However, even as Christians, we are never to lose the "fear of God."

There are many definitions of the fear of God in the scriptures. One is from Proverbs 8:13: *"To fear the Lord is to hate evil. I hate pride and arrogance, evil behavior and perverse speech."* Also, the fear of the Lord is the realization that God sees everything we do. We realize that we must answer to Him for our actions, and most importantly, we don't want to bring dishonor to His name. Joseph feared God and rejected pleasure with Potiphar's wife. Genesis 39:10 says, *"And though she spoke to Joseph day after day, he refused to go to bed with her or even be with her."* This of course was a refusal to sin against his master, Potiphar. But Joseph also called it a "sin against God."

However, living righteously does not always have good consequences in the immediate future. You will see this in what happens next to Joseph.

---

2. How is Joseph falsely accused? Describe what happens in verses 11-20.

3. Joseph's life had gotten better for a while, but now he enters a time of more injustice. Let's think for a moment about what emotions Joseph might be feeling. First he experienced his brothers' hatred and violence which led to slavery. Then his life became more hopeful when his master Potiphar treated him with kindness and honor. Now, once again, his situation becomes bad as he is unjustly accused and thrown into prison.

   What do you think Joseph might have been thinking as he entered the prison on his first day there?

   How do you feel when injustices happen to you? Do you become angry with God? Do you lose hope for your future? How can you keep from going into despair?

4. How does God show His kindness to Joseph in prison? (Verses 21-23)

Read Genesis 40:1-4.

5. Who is thrown into prison with Joseph in these verses?

While they are in prison, both men have disturbing dreams which Joseph interprets for them. He says that the cupbearer will be restored to his position, but the baker will be executed. Both dreams come true, just as he had said they would. (Genesis 40:5-13)

Read Genesis 40:14-15 and 20-23.

6. What does Joseph ask the cupbearer to do for him when he gets out of prison? (Verse 14)

   Does he do it? (Verse 23)

Read Genesis 41:1-8.

7. How much time has passed since the cupbearer got out of prison?

   Discuss what it must have been like for Joseph to wait in prison day after day for the cupbearer to remember him.

   What do you think God may have been teaching him during this time?

8. Briefly describe the two dreams that Pharaoh had. (Verses 1-7) Were any of his magicians able to interpret them for him? (Verse 8)

Finally the cupbearer remembers Joseph and how he correctly interpreted his dream and the baker's dream. At last he fulfills his promise and speaks to Pharaoh on Joseph's behalf. Pharaoh has Joseph brought in and tells him his two dreams. Joseph says that God is showing Pharaoh what He is about to do. (Genesis 41:9-24)

Read Genesis 41:25-36.

9. What did the seven fat cows and seven healthy heads of grain represent? (Verses 26 & 29)

    What did the seven thin cows and seven empty heads of grain represent? (Verses 27 & 30)

    What did Joseph recommend that Pharaoh should do? (Verses 33-36)

Read Genesis 41:37-45.

10. How did Joseph's situation very suddenly change? What is his new position in Egypt? (Verse 41)

    How do you think his responsibilities while in prison may have helped to prepare him for this important job? (Look back at Genesis 39:22-23)

Read Genesis 41:46-57.

11. How is God blessing Joseph?

12. How is Joseph blessing people from many nations? (Verse 57)

What does this mean for us today?
Application and Prayer

In this study we see how Joseph resisted the temptation to immoral actions with Potiphar's wife, even though she tempted him many times. In the New Testament, the Apostle Paul gives us some warnings regarding sexual temptations.

Read 1 Corinthians 6:18 and 2 Timothy 2:22.

1) What does Paul say we should do when we are faced with sexual temptation?

    How did Joseph do this in Genesis 39:9-12?

2) Temptation itself is not sin. But if we give ourselves the opportunity to consider the sin, to think about it and desire it, we will find it very hard to say no to it.

What do you see in Joseph's words and actions in response to temptation that show that he was doing everything he could to avoid sin? (Look again at Genesis 39:8-10.)

3) In Joseph's situation, he suffers imprisonment for doing what is right. This is a hard thing. But even in prison, *God blesses him!* Now think of what probably would have happened if he had given in to the temptation. He probably would have been caught eventually, and sent to prison. But do you think he would have received the same blessing from God?

How is Joseph's example an encouragement to you?

Read 1 Corinthians 10:13.

4) Think about the temptations that you face—not just sexual temptations, but all of the different temptations that come to you. How does this verse encourage you to resist your temptations?

Take some time now to pray. Ask God to teach you how to find the way of escape when you face temptation.

Before the next study, read Genesis chapters 42-50.

If you are not able to read all of this, at least read Genesis chapter 42 through chapter 46:6 and chapter 50:15-26. This is a lot to read, but it's a wonderful story and all of it is important to understanding the life of Joseph.

Dear friends,
I urge you as foreigners and exiles,
to abstain from sinful desires
which wage war against your soul.
Live such good lives among the pagans that,
though they accuse you of wrong doing,
they may see your good deeds
and glorify God on the day He visits us.

1Peter 2:11-12

13. JOSEPH: A MAN OF FAITH AND FORGIVENESS, Part 3, Genesis 42-50

Opening Questions:

From the last study, tell briefly the unjust events that happened to Joseph. Why was he thrown in prison? How did he finally get released from prison? How did God show Joseph that He was with him, even in prison? What natural disaster did the people of Egypt and the surrounding nations suffer? How did Joseph prepare the people of Egypt for this hard time?

Introduction:

In this study we will see how God will move to bring about the next part of His plan to raise up a nation and teach them His ways. Remember that God told Abraham that He would give the land of Canaan to his offspring as their inheritance. Now, three generations later, they own only a very tiny parcel of the land. God has not forgotten His promise, but there are still many steps the children of Abraham must go through first. In Genesis 15:13-14 God told Abraham that his descendants would be sojourners in a foreign land for 400 years. In this study, we will see how they go to live in that foreign land.

In Canaan, where Jacob and his 11 remaining sons are living, the famine is severe, just as it is in Egypt. Jacob's family needs food. He sends 10 of the sons to Egypt to buy grain. Benjamin, the youngest, however, he does not send. Why? Because Joseph and Benjamin are the only two of Jacob's sons that were born to him by Rachel, the wife he loved, and both were born in his old age. Rachel is now dead, and as far as he knows, Joseph is also dead. He cannot think of losing Benjamin also. (Genesis 42:1-5)

Read Genesis 42:6-9.

1. When his brothers arrive in Joseph's presence, what is the first thing they do? (Verse 6) Do the brothers recognize each other? (Verse 8) What does Joseph immediately remember? (Verse 9)

2. What does Joseph accuse them of? (Verse 9)

Joseph speaks harshly to the brothers and puts them in prison for three days.

Read Genesis 42:18-28.

3. What does Joseph order his brothers to do to prove they are not spies? (Verses 19-20) Why do they think they are suffering these

things? (Verses 21-22)

Why do you think Joseph wept when he heard what they said? (Verses 23-24)

4. In spite of the harsh way he has treated them, how does Joseph now show kindness to his brothers? (Verse 25)
What do you think Joseph is feeling in his heart toward his brothers?

The brothers are filled with guilt.

Notice how the roles have reversed. In the past, Joseph's brothers treated him harshly and refused to listen to his pleas for mercy. Now they are at his mercy (though they don't yet know it is Joseph) and they are filled with fear. On the way home, they discover that the price of the food has been returned in their sacks of grain. They fear they will be accused of being thieves. It is clear from verses 21-22 and later verse 28 that they are still filled with guilt many years after their evil treatment of Joseph. They think that God is punishing them.

The brothers return to their father and report all that has happened. He refuses to allow Benjamin to go to Egypt. Simeon is left in prison in Egypt. Then the food they have bought runs out and Jacob tells his sons they must return to Egypt to buy more food. However, they know they cannot return without bringing Benjamin with them. Jacob finally agrees to send Benjamin with them. He also sends many gifts from the produce of Canaan, as well as the money that was returned in their sacks and money to buy more food. When they arrive, Joseph has them taken to his home. (Genesis 42:29-43:17)

Read Genesis 43:18.

5. Again the brothers are filled with guilt and fear. Why do they think they are being taken to Joseph's house?

Read Genesis 43:26-28.

6. What action do the brothers do before Joseph two times in these verses?

Twenty-two years have passed since Joseph had his dreams. What do you think he must be thinking now? What would you think if you were in his place?

When Joseph sees his younger brother, he is overcome with emotion. He provides a feast for his brothers and has Benjamin given five times the portions of the others. Once again the brothers are sent on their way with their money returned in their sacks. Joseph also orders that his personal silver cup be secretly placed in Benjamin's sack, along with the money. The brothers have not gone far when Joseph sends his steward after them in search of the cup. To the brothers' alarm, the cup is discovered in Benjamin's sack. In great grief the brothers return. Joseph says that Benjamin must stay and serve him as his slave. Judah pleads with Joseph to keep him (Judah) as a slave rather than Benjamin. Finally Joseph can keep his secret no longer. (Genesis 43:29-44:34)

Read Genesis 45:1-15.

(This passage is one of the most moving dramas in all of the scriptures. If you are with a group, you may want to have two people read it. One person can read Joseph's part. This person should read the part with all the emotion that Joseph is showing. The other person should read the other parts that Joseph does not say.)

7. Read again verses 5-7. Who does Joseph say in reality is the One who has sent him to Egypt? Why did He send Joseph there?

8. Joseph reveals himself to his brothers with much loud weeping. Why do you think Joseph is so emotional?

9. Benjamin, who was the only other son of Joseph's mother, Rachel, also wept. (Note: Benjamin was very young and was not with his brothers when they sold Joseph to the traders. He probably did not know what had really happened to his brother.)

   What do you think the other brothers might have been thinking at this time? (Verses 14-15, see also verse 3.)

   Why do you think it might have been hard for them to believe that this was really their brother Joseph?

10. Although Joseph never uses the word "forgive" in this passage, do you think he has forgiven his brothers? If so, why do you think that?

    How does Joseph see God's goodness in all the bad things that have happened to him?

Joseph now sends the brothers back to Canaan to bring their father, their wives and their children to Egypt to live until the end of the famine. He promises to provide well for them. Pharaoh also promises them the best the land has to offer. And so Jacob (also known as Israel), his twelve sons and all their families make their home in the land of Egypt. (Genesis 45:16-47:27)

Seventeen years pass and Jacob (Israel) is approaching death. He calls Joseph to him and makes him swear to bury him with his fathers in Canaan. This seems to be a sign of his faith that God will indeed give his offspring this same land, just as He has promised. After this, he blesses Joseph's two sons, and then gives a blessing to each of his own twelve sons. Genesis 50 tells how Joseph and his brothers go with a great company from Egypt to bury their father in the land of promise. (Genesis 47:28-50:14)

After they return, Joseph's brothers become nervous.

Read Genesis 50:15-21.

11. What were the brothers afraid of? (Verse 15) What message did they send to Joseph? (Verses 16-17)

    What did Joseph do when he heard this? (Verse 17) Why do you think he responded this way?

12. When they meet Joseph face to face, what do the brothers do and say? (verse 18)

    What do you think this shows about them? Do you think they are truly grieved over their actions, or are they merely acting out of fear now that they are vulnerable?

    Why do you think it is so hard for them to believe that Joseph has forgiven them?

13. Read again Joseph's response to them in verses 19-21. This is one of the most beautiful examples of forgiveness in the Scriptures. Discuss some of the things you see that Joseph has learned through the years of hardship since he was sold by his brothers. How does Joseph feel about all that has happened to him?

How can good come out of evil?

Joseph has learned to see the events of life from God's perspective. He does not pretend that his brothers' attitudes and actions were right. Instead, he sees that God took something that men intended for evil and turned it around to use for good. It took many years for Joseph to see what that good was. In the meantime, he continued to faithfully walk with God and trust his future to Him. During the many years he spent suffering injustice, loneliness, prison, and hardship, Joseph grew to trust that God is love, even when men treat each other with hatred and violence. He learned the important lesson that forgiveness from the heart is the path to peace with God, with yourself, and with others.

The Apostle Paul wrote about this in his letter to the Romans. Read Romans 8:28. Now read it again. God is sovereignly in control of everything, and He can turn bad things around to use them for good in our lives and the lives of others. Will you trust Him when bad things come into your life?

Read Genesis 50:24-26.

14. In these verses, what does Joseph say to his brothers that shows that he believes that God will be faithful to His covenant promise?

Although we have no record of God directly speaking His covenant promise to Joseph, it surely must have been told to him by his father. Hebrews 11:22 tells us that Joseph, like Abraham, had faith that God would do what He had said.

What does this mean for us today?
Application and Prayer
Read Romans 12:19-21.

1) Discuss some of the ways that Joseph is a beautiful example of someone who did what this passage says.

2) Have there been times in your life when you were treated wrongly by others? Did you plan revenge? Did you hold bitterness in your heart? Or did you trust God to make things right in His way and in His time?

   If not, what will you do differently in the future?

3) Discuss examples of practical ways that you can overcome evil with good.

4) Often it is not easy for us to obey these verses. It is not natural for us to show kindness to those who treat us with hatred or cruelty. But we must remember that as believers, we have the Holy Spirit living inside of us. He promises to help us in our weakness.

   Take some time now to pray and ask God to give you His grace to show love to your enemies. If there are specific incidents in your life where people have wronged you, talk to Him about those now.

A CHALLENGE...

If you are able to, before the next study read through the entire book of Genesis (chapters 1-50) once again. It will probably take you a total of 4 or 5 hours. It is best if you can do this all at one time. If you can't do it all at one time, try to read it all over 3 or 4 sessions. Don't read so fast that you can't understand what's happening, but don't stop to meditate on one or two verses either. This time, you are reading to get the "big picture," that is, to see how all of the various stories flow together.

One idea that you might find enjoyable is to gather as a small group for an entire morning or evening (or you may want to do this in two separate sessions) and take turns reading out loud. All who want to and are good readers can read a chapter at a time. Those who are listening will need to be careful not to fall asleep or let their minds wander!

It may not be easy to set aside this much time, and you may find it challenging to concentrate for this long. But you will find it very rewarding if you do it!

14. OVERVIEW FROM CREATION TO JOSEPH
Genesis 1-50

Opening Questions:

From our previous study, what are some of the ways that Joseph showed mercy to his brothers? Why were they full of fear? Who did Joseph say had really brought him to Egypt? For what purpose did He bring him there?

Introduction:

Did you take the challenge at the end of the last study? If you did, you will be better prepared for this study. This one is different from the others. Instead of looking at one or two people or events, this time we will take a broad look at the whole book of Genesis to see some of the important lessons that we learn from it. Don't rush this study! You may want to take more than one session to go through it so you can take time to recall many of the wonderful truths you have learned from Genesis.

I. From Genesis 1 and 2:

1. What do we learn about the creation of the world from these chapters?

2. What do we learn about the creation of mankind?

3. How do the truths found here encourage you to believe in God's love for you and care of you?

    How do they help you to believe that God has a purpose for the world and for every person?

When I look at your heavens, the work of your fingers, the moon and the stars, which you have set in place, what is man that you are mindful of him, and the son of man that you care for him? Yet you have made him a little lower than the heavenly beings and crowned him with glory and honor. You have given him dominion over the works of your hands; you have put all things under his feet. (Psalm 8:3-6, ESV)

"You are worthy, our Lord and God, to receive glory and honor and power, for you created all things, and by your will they were created and have their being." (Revelation 4:11)

II. From Genesis 3:

1. What were the consequences of Adam and Eve's disobedience? (verses 7-8; 16-19; and 21-24)
2. Is God responsible for the evil that we see in the world today? Explain your answer.
3. What did God do to cover Adam and Eve's shame? (verse 21)
4. How does God cover our shame?

"See, I lay a stone in Zion, a chosen and precious Cornerstone, and the one who trusts in Him will never be put to shame." (1Peter 2:6)

III. From Genesis 4-9:

1. Explain the condition of man on the earth as the years went by. What happened to God's perfect creation?
2. According to chapters 6-7, what did God do because of this condition?
3. Why did God spare Noah? (Genesis 6:8, 9 and 22)
4. How do these chapters help you to understand why God brings judgment? What do people today need to do to escape destruction in the final judgment in the same way that Noah was saved from the flood?

For God so loved the world that he gave his one and only Son, that whoever believes in him shall not perish but have eternal life. (John 3:16)

Just as people are destined to die once, and after that to face judgment, so Christ was sacrificed once to take away the sins of many; and he will appear a second time, not to bear sin, but to bring salvation to those who are waiting for him. (Hebrews 9:27-28)

IN GENESIS 1 – 11...

...we learn about creation and man's disobedience. We see how sin increased and how God brought judgment through the flood. However, we see from Genesis 3:15 that God had a plan from the very beginning to destroy the power of mankind's enemy, Satan.

IN GENESIS 12 – 50...

... we see God, in His great mercy, beginning to bring about this plan. We see Him calling out Abraham and his offspring to be His specially chosen people. In the next part of this study we will look at some of the things that we have learned from Abraham, Isaac, Jacob, and Joseph.

V. Abraham and Isaac

1. Read God's promise to Abraham in Genesis 12:1-3 and also in Genesis 15:1-5. Why was Abraham (Abram) counted righteous before God? (Genesis 15:6)

    How did Abraham show that he had faith?

By faith Abraham, when called to go to a place he would later receive as his inheritance, obeyed and went, even though he did not know where he was going. By faith he made his home in the promised land like a stranger in a foreign country; he lived in tents, as did Isaac and Jacob, who were heirs with him of the same promise. For he was looking forward to the city with foundations, whose architect and builder is God. And by faith even Sarah, who was past childbearing age, was enabled to bear children because she considered him faithful who had made the promise. And so from this one man, and he as good as dead, came descendants as numerous as the stars in the sky and as countless as the sand on the seashore. (Hebrews 11:8-12)

    How are we today counted righteous before God?

The words "it was credited to him [Abraham]" were written not for him alone, but also for us, to whom God will credit righteousness—for us who believe in him who raised Jesus our Lord from the dead. (Romans 4:23-24)

2. Describe the covenant that God made with Abraham. (Genesis 17:1-10)

Throughout the rest of the Old Testament, God will be teaching the offspring of Abraham—the nation of Israel, how to live as people of the covenant. He will teach them how to live as His people and worship Him as their only God.

3. Tell how Abraham showed that he feared God and that he trusted Him when God tested him in Genesis 22.

By faith Abraham, when God tested him, offered Isaac as a sacrifice. He who had embraced the promises was about to sacrifice his one and only son, even though God had said to him, "It is through Isaac that your offspring will be reckoned." Abraham reasoned that God could even raise the dead, and so in a manner of speaking he did receive Isaac back from death. (Hebrews 11:17-19)

4. How does the story of Abraham's life help you to understand a little better that God is a faithful God?

V. Jacob

1. Do you remember what the name "Jacob" means? In your own words, tell how Jacob's name suited him. (Genesis 25:29-34 and Genesis 27)
2. How did God use Jacob's Uncle Laban to humble him? (Genesis 29:16-30; Genesis 30:25-36; and Genesis 31:6-7)
3. How did God show His faithfulness to Jacob during the years that he was away from his father's home?
4. As God patiently worked in Jacob's life, what changes took place in him? (Genesis 32:9-10; Genesis 33:18-20; Genesis 35:3

    What new name did God give him? (Genesis 32:28; Genesis 35:9)

...for it is God who works in you, both to will and to work for his good pleasure. (Philippians 2:13, ESV)

VI. Joseph

1. Briefly tell some of the unjust incidents that happened to Joseph. (Genesis 37:23-28; Genesis 39:6-20; and Genesis 40:23 and 41:1)
2. Describe some of the ways that Joseph is a good example for us. (See Genesis 39:6-20, Genesis 45:4-8, and Genesis 50:15-21)

And we know that in all things God works for the good of those who love him, who have been called according to his purpose. (Romans 8:28)

3. How is Joseph's life a good example of the above verse? (Genesis 45:4-8 and Genesis 50:15-21)

4. Remember that in Genesis 15:13-14 the Lord prophesied to Abraham that his offspring would be strangers in Egypt for 400 years. In Genesis 46:1-4 He repeats this word. How did God sovereignly move in the life of Joseph to fulfill this prophecy?

As you continue on in your study of God's Word you will see that:

- As He promised, God will make Abraham's descendants into a great nation.
- Although many times they will be rebellious, God will continually work with them to teach them to walk in His ways.
- Through His people, God will display His power and glory to the surrounding nations.
- God is preparing His people for the coming of the Savior. Finally, in just the right time, God will send His Son, Jesus, the Messiah, to save all people from their sins.

Take a few minutes now to think about and discuss the following questions with your group. If you are studying alone, write down your thoughts in a journal.

From your study of the book of Genesis, what touched you the most?

What lessons have you learned personally that have changed you in some way?

To Do on Your Own

Below are suggestions of several studies you may want to do which are not included in this book. You could read them alone, or someone in your group could guide your discussion with the same type of questions that are used in this book. Such questions will help you to look closely at the passages and discuss how to apply the truths to your lives in today's world.

Abraham and Isaac with kings
Genesis 12:10-20; Genesis 20; Genesis 26:6-11

Abraham had several encounters with kings where he acted deceptively. He called his wife Sarah "my sister." On both occasions, he was afraid that the king would kill him and take her as his wife. Actually, they did take Sarah because he called her his sister. Abraham used deception to protect himself, which put Sarah in a very difficult place. The Lord intervened to protect Sarah's purity.

Years later, Isaac followed his father's example with another king named Abimelek. (Abimelek means "my father the king" which was probably not a name but a title for kings in those days, similar to the word "Pharaoh.") Isaac, following his father's habit, called Rebekah his sister. Again God intervened and saved her purity. The writer of Genesis tells us that the kings rebuked Abraham and Isaac for their deception.

The Bible makes clear that all people... prophets, kings, and ordinary people... have fallen short of God's glory. All need salvation by God's grace. No one will appear before God in his own righteousness. Only Jesus Christ lived a perfect life before God. In these studies we see a family weakness that began with Abraham and came out in other children born later: deception. Such deception caused problems many times in the family of Abraham. And so it is with us. The habits we form are often seen in our children when they grow up. As followers of Jesus, we must learn God's ways and put off our old ways. None of these great men of faith were perfect. Yet, God was teaching them His ways and continuing His covenant with them. They continued to walk with Him by faith.

ABRAHAM AND LOT
Genesis 13 and 14

These two chapters tell of two important interactions between Abraham and Lot. Chapter 13 tells how Lot separates from Abraham and moves to the lower plain, leaving Abraham to dwell in the higher, less fertile areas. The plain looks more appealing to Lot, but as you see in chapter 14 and then in Study 7 (Genesis 18-19), this is not necessarily a better place to live. In Genesis 14, Abraham has to rescue his nephew from a group of kings who have come in and attacked his city. Studying these chapters before doing Study 7 will help you understand how Lot got himself into the situation he was in. It will also help you to see that choosing the easy life is often not the best way to grow in our walk with God.

A WIFE FOR ISAAC
Genesis 24

This is a very touching and romantic story! You will remember that God called Abraham to leave the land of his relatives and journey to a new land that He would show to him. Abraham now lives in Canaan. But he doesn't want his son to take a wife from among the Canaanite women. So he sends his servant to the land of his relatives, to the home of his brother, to bring back a wife for Isaac. In this beautiful story we see how the servant prays as he travels, asking God to lead him to the wife of His choice. This chapter will encourage you to seek God's guidance in the important decisions you must make in life. You will see that you can trust Him to lead you in ways that will fulfill His purposes and also bring blessing to your life.

JUDAH AND TAMAR
Genesis 38

As you can see as you study through the book of Genesis, not everyone whom God used for His purposes acted according to God's righteous ways. Some people think that a story of immoral behavior should not be included in a holy book. But in the Old Testament, God allows us to see people as they really were. God was working in history to build a nation that would follow Him and He did it through ordinary people, just like us who live in the world today. God is still working in this world through people—both good and bad—to bring about his purposes.

In this chapter we see that Judah, one of Jacob's twelve sons, cheats his daughter-in-law out of her legitimate right to children. In Jewish culture at that time, if a husband died leaving no children, it was the responsibility of the husband's brother to take the widow as a wife—even if he was already married—and give her children. Tamar is left as a widow and deceived into thinking she will be given to Judah's youngest son. But she is not given to him. Without a husband or a son to protect and care for her, Tamar is left defenseless.

In this story we see Judah's selfishness and also his self-righteousness. He is quick to accuse Tamar of sin without acknowledging his own sin—until his sin is exposed. But God sees Tamar in her helpless situation and blesses her with twin sons. In spite of the circumstances, Judah and one of the twins (Perez) will be a part of the line of the ancestors of Jesus the Messiah. (See Matthew 1:2-3 and Luke 3:33.)

Throughout the Old Testament there is often no comment made by the writer about whether a person's actions were right or wrong. Therefore, we must discern this by looking at the whole of Scripture, as well as at the culture of the time it was written. Certainly, everything in this story is not done in God's way. Yet we see God showing mercy to Tamar. God has said He will be the defender of the defenseless.

GUIDELINES FOR TRANSLATORS

You will note that these studies have been written in simple English. It is our hope that speakers of many different languages will find them easy to translate into their own language. It is not necessary to ask permission before translating them. However, if you do translate them, we would like to know about it. It may be possible for us to include your translation on our website (**www.learnhisways.com**) in the future. You may contact us through our website or by email: **learnhisways@gmail.com**.

We also ask that you follow the guidelines given below in translating. These will help to keep the studies as close as possible to the Scriptures and to the original design of the writers of the study. The suggestions for what words to use are especially important if these studies are to be used with those who are not yet believers. For example, in cultures that are sometimes hostile to the Christian faith, a better word choice can build a bridge instead of raising a barrier to their coming to faith.

Guidelines:

1. **Use actual words from the Bible for direct quotes.**

    Anytime there is anything in quotes, if it is taken from the Bible, please go to the Bible in your own language and copy directly what is there. Do not translate from the English quote. Also, as you are translating a study, keep the Bible in your language open to the passage being studied, and try to use the same terms that are used in that passage as much as possible. For example, in study 6 there is discussion of Abram learning to worship. He made sacrifices on an "altar." Be sure to use the word in your Bible for "altar," not a word you find in the dictionary.

2. **Words to use for "Bible," "Christian," "God" and "Christ."**

    Even though these are studies in Genesis, they speak to Christians and often take the reader to the New Testament for application. However, we are aware that they will also be used by believers who share them with unbelievers.

    In some countries (especially Muslim countries), using the words above or some form of these words can cause unnecessary anger and offense. Some people still think about religious wars when they hear these words, and they associate them with their enemies. Therefore, in your translating please think carefully about the words that you use.

For the word "Bible," use words from your language for "Holy Book," "The Word," God's Word," or "Old or New Testament." In many Muslim countries, "Injil" is a good word to use for "New Testament." For the word "God," you should choose the word that is most commonly used by believers in your country. Believers in some Muslim countries use the word "Allah," other countries have other words that they prefer.

For "Christ," it's best to use the word in your language for "Messiah," or "Anointed One." This is the meaning of the word "Christ." For "Christian," use words from your language for "follower of Jesus the Messiah," "follower of Jesus," or "believer"-- or whatever words are most commonly used and accepted by believers in your country.

If you are translating into a language with a Christian heritage, obviously you should use the words they are familiar with. In general, please try to choose words for these terms that are familiar, easily understood for their true meaning, and least likely to cause unnecessary offense.

3. Use simple language.

We have tried to use simple sentences in the English to make these Bible studies easy to understand for anyone, including those who have no knowledge of the Bible and those who have limited education. We want them to be a help to ALL people—not just those who already know a lot. These studies have been used successfully with those who are not yet believers, as well as with very mature believers.

Please keep this in mind in translating. Some languages commonly use very complex and formal language in writing. We would ask that these studies be translated into language that sounds just the way people talk in normal, everyday life. They have been written for group discussion, therefore, it is important that everyone understand the questions and comments. Our goal is to help people understand the Bible, not to make them confused.

4. Have someone check the translation.

To make these studies as accurate as possible in your native language, have a native speaker who is also fluent in English do the first translation **from the English.** Then, have a native English speaker who is also fluent in your language check the translation. In the final step, the original translator and the English checker should discuss any questions in the translation and come to an agreement on the best wording.

Keep this in mind... As you go through the translation process, if there is anything in the studies that is unclear, feel free to contact us through our website (www.learnhisways.com) **or by email** (learnhisways@gmail.com).

God bless you as you translate. We trust the Lord will use these studies to strengthen the Body of Christ in many different language groups around the world.

Made in the USA
Middletown, DE
20 October 2025